A Quick Reference Guide To Understanding Mental Health

A Mental Health Handbook

Pascale Davis and Gregg Davis

A Quick Reference Guide to Understanding Mental Health: A Mental Health Handbook

Published by: Virtual Psychiatric Care / MiamiPsych Concierge, LLC 1900 N Bayshore Drive, Suite 1A Miami, Florida 33132

MEDICAL DISCLAIMER: This handbook is provided strictly for educational and informational purposes and does not constitute medical, psychiatric, or psychological advice, diagnosis, or treatment. Always seek the advice of a qualified mental health professional or physician with any questions you may have regarding a medical or mental health condition.

EMERGENCY CONTACT: If you are experiencing a mental health emergency, please call **911** immediately or contact the Suicide and Crisis Lifeline by calling or texting **988**.

NOTE ON CASE STUDIES: All case studies and patient scenarios depicted in this handbook are fictional composites created solely for educational purposes. They do not represent specific individuals, and any resemblance to actual persons, living or deceased, is purely coincidental.

First Edition: 2026 www.VirtualPsychiatricCare.com

Contents

Dedication & Foreword

This book is dedicated to every person who has ever felt alone in their struggle with mental health, and to the families, friends, and partners who stand beside them, even when they don't have the words.

My journey in mental health is deeply personal. It began in 1994 as a young psychiatric nurse, fueled by a passion that only grew over the decades. In 2018, I realized a lifelong dream by opening a private practice to see patients both in person and through the emerging medium of video consultations.

Recognizing the immense need for broader access to care, and with the vision and steadfast support of my husband, Gregg Davis, we evolved that dream into a 100% remote platform: **Virtual Psychiatric Care (VPC)**. Our mission is simple yet vital: to provide access to quality, affordable mental health treatment regardless of geography.

As survivors of complex trauma and depression, we know firsthand that the journey toward healing is neither straight nor short. This personal history has been the driving force behind VPC's growth, fueling our reach across the nation to ensure that no one has to navigate their path to recovery alone. This handbook is a reflection of that commitment, a tool designed to empower you with the language and understanding needed to foster resilience and transformation.

We know that with patience, grace, and the right support, transformation is possible.

— **Pascale Davis, MSN, PMHNP-BC** & **Gregg Davis** Founders, Virtual Psychiatric Care

Introduction

Why This Book Matters

One in five adults in the United States experiences a mental health condition in any given year. Despite this staggering prevalence, mental health remains one of the most misunderstood and stigmatized areas of medicine. People suffer in silence because they do not have the words to describe what they are feeling, because they fear being judged, or because they simply do not know where to turn.

This handbook exists to bridge that gap. It is written for the person lying awake at three in the morning wondering if their racing thoughts are normal. It is written for the parent who suspects their child's struggles go beyond typical growing pains. It is written for the partner who feels helpless watching someone they love retreat from the world. And it is written for anyone who has ever typed their symptoms into a search engine at midnight, looking for answers.

Mental health literacy, the ability to understand, identify, and respond to mental health conditions, is one of the most powerful tools we can put into the hands of the public. Research consistently demonstrates that individuals who understand mental health terminology, recognize symptoms, and know how to access care are more likely to seek treatment early, more likely to support loved ones effectively, and more likely to recover.

How to Use This Book

This handbook is designed to be used in whatever way is most helpful to you. You may read it cover to cover, or you may use it as a reference guide, turning to specific sections as needs arise. The glossary is organized alphabetically for easy reference. The case studies are organized thematically and can be read independently of one another.

We encourage you to share this book with others. Place it in your workplace break room. Give it to a friend who is struggling. Discuss it with your family. The more people who understand mental health, the closer we come to a world where seeking help is as natural as seeing a doctor for a broken bone.

A Note on Language

Language matters in mental health. Throughout this book, we use person-first language wherever possible. We say a person with depression rather than a depressed person because identity is not defined by diagnosis. We also use clinical terminology not to create distance but to empower readers with the precise language that professionals use, so that conversations with providers feel less intimidating and more collaborative.

About Virtual Psychiatric Care

This handbook is brought to you by Virtual Psychiatric Care, an organization dedicated to expanding access to psychiatric services through telehealth. By utilizing secure video consultations, platforms like VPC aim to remove the logistical and emotional barriers that often prevent individuals from beginning their healing journey.

To learn more or to schedule an appointment, visit www.VirtualPsychiatricCare.com

Brief Overview:

Theories of Mental Illness

Why Mental Health Conditions Happen

There is no single cause of most mental health conditions. The simplest modern explanation is that they usually come from a combination of biology, psychology, development, and life circumstances rather than one isolated problem. Major organizations like **National Institute of Mental Health (NIMH)** and **World Health Organization (WHO)** describe mental health as being shaped by interacting genetic, brain, behavioral, social, and environmental factors.

The Biopsychosocial Model

This is still the most practical, easy-to-understand framework. It says mental health conditions can develop through the interaction of three domains:

Biological factors: Genetics, brain circuits, hormones, sleep, inflammation, and medical illness.

Psychological factors: Temperament, coping style, thinking patterns, attachment, and trauma history.

Social factors: Family stress, abuse, poverty, discrimination, isolation, and work or school pressure.

Stress-Vulnerability (Diathesis-Stress) Theory

This theory says some people are born or shaped with a higher vulnerability, and symptoms appear when enough stress builds on top of that vulnerability. In plain language: two people can go through the same event, but the one with more genetic risk, trauma history, or nervous-system sensitivity may be more likely to develop depression, anxiety, PTSD, psychosis, or substance problems.

Developmental and Neurodevelopmental Theories

These theories focus on how the brain and emotional system develop over time. Early childhood experiences, attachment, neglect, trauma, puberty, and adolescent brain development can all affect how a person learns to regulate emotion, handle stress, trust others, and interpret danger. NIMH's developmental work emphasizes that mental disorders often emerge through developmental pathways involving genes, brain function, behavior, and environment interacting over time.

Trauma and Adversity Frameworks

More recent clinical thinking gives much greater weight to trauma, chronic adversity, and nervous-system overload. In this view, some symptoms are understood not simply as "disorders," but as adaptations to overwhelming experiences. Hypervigilance, emotional numbing, dissociation, mistrust, self-harm, and relationship instability can all be understood partly through the effects of trauma and repeated stress on the brain and body.

Social Determinants and Structural Frameworks

One of the biggest modern shifts is recognizing that mental health is also shaped by the conditions in which people live. This includes housing, poverty, food insecurity, violence exposure, discrimination, unstable work, lack of access to care, and unequal access to power and resources. Recent reviews and WHO guidance strongly emphasize that poor mental health is not only an individual problem; it is also influenced by social and structural conditions.

Gene–Environment Interaction

Older thinking sometimes asked, "Is it genes or environment?" Newer research says it is usually both working together. Genes may increase sensitivity, but life experiences can influence whether that vulnerability is activated, reduced, or buffered. In other words, genes may load the gun, but environment often affects whether and how it fires.

Transdiagnostic Frameworks

A newer approach is that many conditions share some of the same core processes. Instead of seeing depression, anxiety, OCD, trauma, and substance problems as fully separate, transdiagnostic models look at overlapping mechanisms such as emotion dysregulation, avoidance, rumination, threat sensitivity, impulsivity, shame, and sleep disruption. This helps explain why people often have more than one diagnosis at the same time.

RDoC and Dimensional Models

NIMH's Research Domain Criteria (RDoC) is one of the main recent research frameworks. It does not replace diagnosis in everyday practice, but it studies mental health problems by looking at core systems such as emotion, cognition, motivation, social processes, and arousal, across levels from genes and brain circuits to behavior and self-report. The idea is that mental health symptoms may be better understood as dimensions of functioning rather than neat boxes.

Network Theory

Another newer framework is network theory. It suggests that some disorders are not caused by one hidden disease process alone, but by symptoms that can trigger and reinforce each other. For example, poor sleep can worsen anxiety, anxiety can increase avoidance, avoidance can worsen isolation, and isolation can deepen depression. Over time, the symptom network can sustain itself.

The Most Practical Bottom Line

The most current overall view is this: mental health conditions usually arise from interacting layers of risk and resilience across the lifespan. Biology matters. Trauma matters. Thinking patterns matter. Relationships matter. Social conditions matter. Development matters. Recent frameworks are moving away from one-cause explanations and toward more integrated models that look at the whole person in context.

Navigating Modern Psychiatric Care:

From "I Need Help" to Getting the Right Help

There is a massive, underserved space between knowing you need help and knowing how to use modern psychiatric systems to actually get the right help. Most people who reach the point of searching for a provider have already spent weeks, months, or even years suffering. They have already overcome the enormous barrier of stigma. They are ready. But the system itself presents a second barrier that is rarely talked about: confusion.

How is online psychiatry different from therapy?

Can a provider really prescribe medication through a screen?

How do you know if a telehealth platform is legitimate?

What should you say in your first appointment?

How do you track whether your treatment is working?

These are not trivial questions. They are the questions that determine whether someone gets meaningful, effective care or falls through the cracks of a system that was not designed with them in mind.

This chapter is designed to close that gap. It is written in plain language for people who are navigating the psychiatric system for the first time, for people returning to care after a break, and for the family members and friends who are helping someone find the right path forward.

How Virtual Psychiatry Differs from Therapy

One of the most common points of confusion is the difference between psychiatry and therapy. They are not the same thing, though they work powerfully together.

Therapy (also called psychotherapy or counseling) is a process of structured conversation with a licensed mental health professional. Therapists help you understand patterns of thinking, feeling, and behaving. They teach coping skills, help you process trauma, improve relationships, and develop insight into your inner world. Common approaches include CBT,

DBT, EMDR, psychodynamic therapy, and many others.

Psychiatry is a medical specialty. Psychiatric providers, including psychiatrists (MDs or DOs) and psychiatric nurse practitioners (PMHNPs), are trained to evaluate mental health conditions from a clinical and biological perspective. They can diagnose conditions, prescribe and manage medications, order lab work, and monitor the physical effects of treatment.

Virtual psychiatry delivers this same psychiatric expertise through secure video consultations rather than in-person office visits. The clinical standard of care is identical. Your provider conducts a full evaluation, makes a diagnosis, develops a treatment plan, prescribes medication when appropriate, and monitors your progress through regular follow-up appointments, all from the privacy of your own home.

The key takeaway: therapy helps you change how you think, feel, and cope. Psychiatry addresses the biological and medical dimensions of your condition, often through medication. Most people benefit from both. Virtual psychiatry makes the medical side of mental health care accessible to anyone with an internet connection.

How Medication Management Works Online

The initial evaluation. Your first appointment with a virtual psychiatric provider is typically 45 to 60 minutes. During this session, your provider conducts a comprehensive psychiatric evaluation including a detailed review of your symptoms, their duration and severity, your medical history, family psychiatric history, any medications you are currently taking, your substance use history, and your goals for treatment.

Prescribing. If medication is recommended, your provider writes an electronic prescription sent directly to the pharmacy of your choice. You are not required to use a specific pharmacy or mail-order service. Your provider will explain the medication, its expected benefits, potential side effects, how long it may take to work, and what to watch for.

Follow-up and monitoring. Effective medication management is an ongoing process. Follow-up appointments are typically every two to four weeks when starting a new medication, then may extend to monthly or quarterly once stability is achieved. During these visits, your provider assesses effectiveness, checks for side effects, adjusts dosages, and may order lab work if needed.

What virtual medication management cannot do. Virtual providers cannot perform physical examinations, draw blood, or administer injections. If your provider needs lab results, they will order them and direct you to a local lab. Certain controlled substances may have prescribing restrictions in some states for telehealth.

How to Evaluate a Telehealth Provider

Not all telehealth platforms are created equal. Knowing what to look for can mean the difference between getting meaningful care and wasting time and money.

Check credentials and specialization.

Your provider should be board-certified or licensed in their field. For psychiatric care, look for psychiatrists (MD or DO) or psychiatric mental health nurse practitioners (PMHNP-BC). Verify that the platform specializes in mental health.

Verify state licensure.

Telehealth providers must be licensed in the state where you are physically located at the time of your appointment.

Evaluate the depth of the initial evaluation.

A thorough first appointment should last at least 45 minutes. If a platform promises a prescription in under 15 minutes without a real evaluation, that is a red flag.

Understand the continuity model.

Will you see the same provider at every visit? Continuity of care is one of the most important factors in effective psychiatric treatment.

Ask about communication between visits.

A good platform offers a way to message your provider or clinical team between visits.

Review the subscription and fee structure.

Understand what you are paying for and whether the platform accepts your insurance.

Red Flags to Avoid in Online Psychiatric Care

Rushed evaluations. If your first appointment lasts less than 15 minutes and ends with a prescription, the evaluation was almost certainly inadequate.

No follow-up plan. A provider who prescribes medication without scheduling follow-up is not practicing responsible medicine.

Inability to choose or keep your provider. If the platform assigns a different provider at every visit, your care becomes fragmented.

Pressure to use a specific pharmacy. You should always have the right to send your prescription to the pharmacy of your choice.

No crisis plan or emergency guidance. A responsible provider will discuss what to do in a crisis and provide emergency contact information.

Marketing that sounds too good to be true. Promises like "get your prescription today" prioritize speed over safety.

Providers who do not specialize in psychiatry. Mental health is a specialty. Treat it like one.

How to Prepare for a Virtual Psychiatric Appointment

Before your first appointment:

Write down your symptoms. Include what you are experiencing, when it started, how often it occurs, and how it affects your daily life. Be specific.

Prepare your history. Know your medical history, current medications (including supplements), family history of mental health conditions, and any previous psychiatric treatment.

Identify your goals. What do you want to get out of treatment? Better sleep? Reduced anxiety? Improved focus? Fewer mood swings?

Set up your environment. Choose a quiet, private space with a stable internet connection. Treat this appointment with the same seriousness you would give an in-person medical visit.

During the appointment:

Be honest. Your provider cannot help you effectively if they do not have accurate information. There is no judgment in a psychiatric evaluation.

Ask questions. If your provider recommends a medication, ask what it does, how long it takes to work, what side effects to expect, and what to do if you experience problems.

Take notes. Write down the name of any medication prescribed, the dosage, when to take it, and when your next appointment is.

How to Track Symptoms and Communicate Effectively with Your Provider

One of the most powerful things you can do for your own mental health care is to become an active participant in tracking your symptoms.

What to track:

Mood: Rate your overall mood daily on a simple scale of 1 to 10. Note patterns.

Sleep: Record what time you go to bed, when you fall asleep, how many times you wake up, and what time you get up.

Energy and motivation: Note days when fatigue makes basic tasks feel impossible versus days when you feel functional.

Anxiety and panic: Record episodes, triggers, and duration.

Side effects: Track any changes that began after starting or adjusting a medication.

Life events: Major stressors, conflicts, losses, or changes in routine can significantly affect your symptoms.

How to communicate effectively:

Lead with the most important information. Summarize trends rather than reading every data point. Structured communication transforms a follow-up from a vague check-in into a targeted clinical conversation.

How to Integrate Digital Tools with Real Clinical Care

We live in an era where mental health apps, meditation platforms, online support groups, AI chatbots, and wellness influencers are everywhere. The key is understanding what digital tools can and cannot do.

What digital tools can do well:

Symptom tracking apps, meditation and mindfulness apps, online psychoeducation from reputable sources, and peer support communities can all complement professional care.

What digital tools cannot do:

No app can diagnose you. No chatbot can prescribe medication. No influencer can replace a board-certified psychiatric provider who has evaluated your specific history, biology, and needs.

The integration principle:

Professional psychiatric treatment provides the clinical foundation. Digital tools build on that foundation by supporting your daily well-being between appointments. They work best together, and neither fully replaces the other.

At Virtual Psychiatric Care, we encourage our patients to use tools that support their treatment goals. The goal is not to choose between technology and clinical care. The goal is to use both wisely.

Psychiatric Medications: What to Expect

Understanding psychiatric medications helps you feel more confident about treatment. Here's what you need to know about the most common medication classes:

Antidepressants

Antidepressants treat depression, anxiety disorders, OCD, PTSD, and some chronic pain conditions.

SSRIs (Selective Serotonin Reuptake Inhibitors): Most commonly prescribed antidepressants. Examples: Zoloft (sertraline), Lexapro (escitalopram), Prozac (fluoxetine), Celexa (citalopram), Paxil (paroxetine).

How they work: Increase serotonin levels in the brain, improving mood and reducing anxiety.

Timeline: May take 4-6 weeks to feel full effects. Start low and increase gradually to minimize side effects.

Common side effects: Nausea, headache, sleep changes, sexual side effects. Most side effects improve after the first few weeks.

SNRIs (Serotonin-Norepinephrine Reuptake Inhibitors): Examples: Effexor (venlafaxine), Cymbalta (duloxetine), Pristiq (desvenlafaxine).

How they work: Increase both serotonin and norepinephrine, helpful for depression with low energy and chronic pain conditions.

Timeline and side effects: Similar to SSRIs.

Atypical Antidepressants: Examples: Wellbutrin (bupropion), Remeron (mirtazapine), Trintellix (vortioxetine).

Wellbutrin: Increases dopamine and norepinephrine. Doesn't cause sexual side effects or weight gain. Often used for depression with fatigue or to help with smoking cessation.

Remeron: Increases serotonin and norepinephrine. Helpful for depression with insomnia and poor appetite. Can cause increased appetite and drowsiness.

Anti-Anxiety Medications

Benzodiazepines: Examples: Xanax (alprazolam), Klonopin (clonazepam), Ativan (lorazepam), Valium (diazepam).

How they work: Rapid relief of acute anxiety

symptoms by enhancing GABA (calming neuro-transmitter).

Usage: Typically prescribed short-term or as-needed due to tolerance and dependence risk. Very effective for panic attacks, acute anxiety, and sleep.

Important considerations: Can be habit-forming with long-term use. Shouldn't be stopped abruptly. Not recommended as first-line treatment for chronic anxiety.

Buspirone: Non-benzodiazepine anti-anxiety medication. Takes several weeks to work. No addiction potential. Helpful for generalized anxiety disorder.

Hydroxyzine (Vistaril): Antihistamine with anti-anxiety properties. Works quickly, non-addictive. Used as needed for anxiety or sleep.

Mood Stabilizers

Used primarily for bipolar disorder to prevent mood episodes.

Lithium: Gold-standard mood stabilizer. Highly effective for bipolar disorder. Requires regular blood tests to monitor therapeutic levels and kidney/thyroid function.

Anticonvulsant Mood Stabilizers: Examples: Depakote (valproic acid), Lamictal (lamotrigine), Tegretol (carbamazepine).

Lamictal: Particularly effective for bipolar depression. Requires slow dose increase to avoid rare but serious rash.

Depakote: Effective for mania. Requires blood level monitoring.

Antipsychotic Medications

Treat psychotic disorders, bipolar disorder, and sometimes used to augment antidepressants for treatment-resistant depression.

Atypical (Second-Generation) Antipsychotics: Examples: Abilify (aripiprazole), Seroquel (quetiapine), Zyprexa (olanzapine), Risperdal (risperidone), Latuda (lurasidone), Rexulti (brexpiprazole).

Uses: Schizophrenia, bipolar disorder, augmentation for depression, severe anxiety, agitation.

Monitoring: Regular metabolic monitoring (weight, blood sugar, cholesterol) as some antipsychotics can affect metabolism.

ADHD Medications

Stimulants: Examples: Adderall (amphetamine), Ritalin/Concerta (methylphenidate), Vyvanse (lisdexamfetamine).

How they work: Increase dopamine and norepinephrine, improving focus, attention, and impulse control.

Forms: Immediate-release (lasts 4-6 hours) or extended-release (lasts 8-12 hours).

Common side effects: Decreased appetite, difficulty sleeping, increased heart rate. Usually managed with timing of doses and lifestyle adjustments.

Non-Stimulant ADHD Medications: Examples: Strattera (atomoxetine), Intuniv (guanfacine), Kapvay (clonidine).

Benefits: No abuse potential, smooth effect throughout day, helpful when stimulants cause side effects or for people with substance use history.

Drawbacks: Take longer to work (2-4 weeks), may be less effective than stimulants for some people.

Sleep Medications

Common Prescriptions:

- Trazodone: Sedating antidepressant, very commonly used off-label for insomnia

- Ambien (zolpidem): Short-acting sleep aid

- Lunesta (eszopiclone): Sleep aid

- Belsomra (suvorexant): Newer mechanism, blocks wakefulness signals

- Remeron: Antidepressant with strong sedating effects

Approach: Providers emphasize sleep hygiene (consistent schedule, limiting screens, cool dark room) alongside medication. Many sleep medications are intended for short-term use while addressing underlying causes.

Medication for Substance Use Disorders

Buprenorphine (Suboxone, Subutex): Treats opioid use disorder by reducing cravings and withdrawal symptoms without producing euphoria. Allows people to stabilize their lives while in recovery.

Naltrexone: Blocks opioid receptors (for opioid use disorder) or reduces alcohol cravings (for alcohol use disorder). Available as daily pill (ReVia) or monthly injection (Vivitrol).

Acamprosate (Campral): Reduces alcohol cravings by normalizing brain chemistry affected by chronic alcohol use.

Part One: The Mental Health Glossary

The Mental Health Glossary

Understanding mental health begins with understanding its language. This comprehensive glossary provides clear, accessible definitions of the terms, conditions, treatments, and concepts you are most likely to encounter in conversations about mental health. Whether you are a patient, a family member, a caregiver, or a professional, this glossary is designed to be your reference companion.

Glossary: A – I

ACT (Acceptance and Commitment Therapy)

A form of psychotherapy that encourages individuals to accept difficult thoughts and feelings rather than fighting or avoiding them, while committing to actions aligned with personal values. ACT uses mindfulness, cognitive defusion, and values-based goal setting. It is effective for depression, anxiety, chronic pain, and substance use disorders.

Acute Stress Disorder (ASD)

A mental health condition that can develop within the first month after a person experiences or witnesses a traumatic event. Symptoms include intrusive memories, dissociation, avoidance behaviors, and heightened arousal. It is distinguished from PTSD by its shorter duration.

ADHD (Attention-Deficit/Hyperactivity Disorder)

A neurodevelopmental disorder characterized

by persistent patterns of inattention, hyperactivity, and impulsivity that interfere with daily functioning and development. It is one of the most commonly diagnosed conditions in children and frequently persists into adulthood.

Adjustment Disorder

A stress-related condition in which a person has difficulty coping with or adjusting to a particular life stressor such as divorce, job loss, illness, or a major life transition. Symptoms typically begin within three months of the stressful event.

Affect

The outward expression of emotion as observed by others. A person's affect can be described as flat, blunted, constricted, labile, or appropriate. Clinicians assess affect during mental status examinations.

Agoraphobia

An anxiety disorder characterized by fear and avoidance of situations where escape might be difficult or help unavailable during a panic attack. This may include open spaces, crowds, public transportation, or being outside of the home alone.

Anhedonia

The inability to experience pleasure from activities that were once enjoyable. It is a core symptom of major depressive disorder and can also appear in schizophrenia, PTSD, and substance use disorders.

Anorexia Nervosa

A serious eating disorder characterized by an intense fear of gaining weight, distorted body image, and severe restriction of food intake leading to dangerously low body weight. It has one of the highest mortality rates of any psychiatric disorder.

Antidepressant

A class of medications used primarily to treat depression, though they are also prescribed for anxiety disorders, OCD, PTSD, chronic pain, and other conditions. Common types include SSRIs, SNRIs, TCAs, and MAOIs.

Antipsychotic

A class of medications used to manage psychotic symptoms such as hallucinations, delusions, and disorganized thinking. They are commonly prescribed for schizophrenia, bipolar disorder, and severe agitation. They are divided into first-generation (typical) and second-generation (atypical) categories.

Anxiolytic

A medication used to reduce anxiety symptoms. Benzodiazepines, buspirone, and certain antihistamines are commonly prescribed anxiolytics. Due to the risk of dependence, these medications require careful monitoring.

ASMR (Autonomous Sensory Meridian Response)

A tingling sensation that typically begins on the scalp and moves down the back of the neck and upper spine, triggered by specific auditory or visual stimuli such as whispering, tapping, or gentle movements. While not a clinical treatment, many individuals report using ASMR content to reduce anxiety, promote relaxation, and improve sleep. Research into its mechanisms and therapeutic applications is still emerging.

Attachment Styles

Patterns of relating to others that develop in early childhood based on interactions with primary caregivers. The four main styles are secure, anxious (preoccupied), avoidant (dismissive), and disorganized (fearful-avoidant). Attachment styles influence how individuals form relationships, handle conflict, respond to intimacy, and manage emotional distress throughout life. Understanding one's attachment style has become a widely discussed framework in therapy and popular mental health content.

Autism Spectrum Disorder (ASD)

A neurodevelopmental condition characterized

by differences in social communication, interaction, and behavior patterns that include restricted or repetitive interests and activities. The spectrum reflects a wide range of abilities and challenges.

Avoidant Personality Disorder

A personality disorder marked by extreme social inhibition, feelings of inadequacy, and hypersensitivity to negative evaluation. Individuals with this condition deeply desire connection but avoid social situations due to fear of rejection.

Behavioral Therapy

A therapeutic approach that focuses on changing unhealthy or self-destructive behaviors by identifying and modifying the environmental triggers and reinforcements that sustain them. It is grounded in learning theory and includes techniques such as exposure therapy and behavioral activation.

Benzodiazepines

A class of psychoactive medications commonly prescribed for anxiety, insomnia, seizures, and muscle relaxation. While effective in the short term, they carry significant risks of tolerance, dependence, and withdrawal, and are generally recommended for short-term use only.

Bipolar Disorder

A mood disorder characterized by alternating episodes of mania (or hypomania) and depression. Bipolar I involves full manic episodes, while Bipolar II involves hypomanic episodes. Both types significantly impact energy levels, activity, sleep, behavior, and the ability to carry out daily tasks.

Body Dysmorphic Disorder (BDD)

A mental health condition in which a person becomes excessively preoccupied with perceived flaws in their physical appearance that are not observable or appear slight to others. This preoccupation causes significant distress and can lead to repetitive behaviors such as mirror checking or excessive grooming.

Borderline Personality Disorder (BPD)

A personality disorder characterized by a pervasive pattern of instability in interpersonal relationships, self-image, emotions, and marked impulsivity. People with BPD often experience intense fear of abandonment, chronic feelings of emptiness, and episodes of anger or self-harm.

Boundaries

The emotional, physical, and psychological limits a person sets to protect their well-being and define how they want to be treated in relationships. Healthy boundaries involve communicating needs clearly, saying no without guilt, and recognizing where one person's responsibility ends and another's begins. In mental health contexts, boundary work is often central to recovery from codependency, enmeshment, people-pleasing, and trauma.

Brainspotting

A therapeutic technique developed by David Grand that uses the client's eye position to locate and process unresolved trauma stored in the brain and body. During a session, the therapist helps the individual find a specific eye position, or "brainspot," that correlates with emotional activation related to a particular issue. By holding that gaze point while maintaining focused mindfulness, the brain's natural healing processes are engaged to reprocess traumatic material. Brainspotting is used for PTSD, anxiety, depression, chronic pain, performance issues, and other conditions rooted in unresolved stress or trauma.

Bulimia Nervosa

An eating disorder characterized by cycles of binge eating followed by compensatory behaviors such as self-induced vomiting, excessive exercise, fasting, or misuse of laxatives. Unlike anorexia, individuals with bulimia may maintain a normal weight.

Burnout

A state of chronic physical and emotional exhaustion resulting from prolonged exposure to work-related or caregiving stress. Symptoms include feeling overwhelmed, emotionally drained, and unable to meet constant demands. While not a formal psychiatric diagnosis, burnout significantly affects mental health and daily functioning.

Catastrophizing

A cognitive distortion in which a person assumes the worst possible outcome will occur. This thinking pattern is common in anxiety disorders and depression and often amplifies feelings of helplessness and dread.

Catatonia

A neuropsychiatric condition characterized by motor abnormalities that may include stupor, rigidity, waxy flexibility, mutism, or purposeless agitation. It can occur in the context of schizophrenia, mood disorders, medical conditions, or medication reactions.

CBT (Cognitive Behavioral Therapy)

An evidence-based psychotherapy approach that helps individuals identify and change negative thought patterns and behaviors that contribute to emotional distress. CBT is widely used for depression, anxiety, PTSD, OCD, and many other mental health conditions.

Circadian Rhythm

The body's internal 24-hour biological clock that regulates the sleep-wake cycle and influences hormone release, body temperature, and mood. Disruptions to circadian rhythm are associated with mood disorders, insomnia, and seasonal affective disorder.

Clinical Depression

See Major Depressive Disorder. The term "clinical depression" is commonly used to distinguish a diagnosable depressive disorder from normal feelings of sadness that are part of the human experience.

Co-Regulation

The process by which one person's calm, safe presence helps another person's nervous system settle and return to a regulated state. Co-regulation is foundational in parent-child relationships, where a caregiver's steady tone, eye contact, and physical warmth help a child learn to manage distress. In adult life, co-regulation continues to play a role in friendships, romantic partnerships, and therapeutic relationships. It is a core concept in polyvagal theory and attachment-informed care.

Codependency

A behavioral pattern in which a person excessively relies on another person for approval, identity, and sense of purpose, often at the expense of their own needs and well-being. Codependent relationships frequently involve enabling behaviors that perpetuate dysfunction.

Cold Exposure Therapy

The practice of using cold water immersion, cold showers, or cryotherapy to activate the body's stress-response system in a controlled way, with the goal of improving mood, reducing inflammation, and building stress resilience. Proponents suggest that brief, intentional cold exposure stimulates the vagus nerve and releases norepinephrine and endorphins. While some research supports mood and alertness benefits, cold exposure should be approached cautiously, especially by individuals with trauma histories or cardiovascular conditions, as it can overstimulate the nervous system.

Comorbidity

The simultaneous presence of two or more disorders or illnesses in the same individual. In mental health, comorbidity is common, as conditions such as depression and anxiety, or substance use and PTSD, frequently co-occur.

Complex PTSD (C-PTSD)

A condition that may develop after exposure to prolonged or repeated traumatic events, particularly those involving interpersonal harm such as childhood abuse, domestic violence, or captivity. In addition to standard PTSD symptoms, C-PTSD includes difficulties with emotional regulation, self-perception, and interpersonal relationships.

Compulsion

A repetitive behavior or mental act that a person feels driven to perform in response to an obsession or according to rigid rules. Compulsions are a hallmark feature of Obsessive-Compulsive Disorder and are performed to reduce anxiety or prevent a feared outcome.

Conversion Disorder

A condition in which psychological stress manifests as neurological symptoms such as blindness, paralysis, tremors, or seizures that cannot be explained by a medical condition. Also known as functional neurological symptom disorder.

Coping Mechanisms

Strategies and behaviors that individuals use to manage stress, emotional pain, or difficult situations. Coping mechanisms can be adaptive, such as exercise, journaling, and seeking social support, or maladaptive, such as substance use, avoidance, or self-harm.

Countertransference

The emotional reactions a therapist may experience toward a patient, often influenced by the therapist's own unresolved psychological issues. Awareness and management of countertransference is essential for effective therapeutic practice.

Couples Therapy

A form of psychotherapy that helps romantic partners improve communication, resolve conflicts, rebuild trust, and strengthen emotional connection. Common approaches include Emotionally Focused Therapy (EFT), which focuses on attachment needs and emotional responsiveness, and the Gottman Method, which emphasizes friendship, conflict management, and shared meaning.

Crisis Intervention

An immediate, short-term form of mental health support designed to help individuals experiencing an acute psychological crisis. The goal is to stabilize the person, reduce immediate distress, and connect them with appropriate ongoing care.

DBT (Dialectical Behavior Therapy)

A specialized form of cognitive behavioral therapy originally developed to treat borderline personality disorder. DBT emphasizes the balance between acceptance and change, teaching skills in mindfulness, distress tolerance, emotional regulation, and interpersonal effectiveness.

Delusion

A fixed, false belief that persists despite evidence to the contrary and is not consistent with the person's cultural background. Common types include persecutory, grandiose, referential, and somatic delusions. Delusions are a key feature of psychotic disorders.

Depersonalization

A dissociative experience in which a person feels detached from their own body, thoughts, or sense of identity, as if observing themselves from outside or feeling that things are not real. It can occur as a standalone disorder or as a symptom of other conditions.

Derealization

A dissociative experience characterized by a persistent or recurrent feeling that one's surroundings are unreal, dreamlike, or visually distorted. Often co-occurs with depersonalization.

Dissociation

A disconnection between a person's thoughts,

identity, consciousness, or memory. Dissociation exists on a spectrum from mild, such as daydreaming, to severe, such as dissociative identity disorder. It often develops as a protective response to trauma.

Dissociative Identity Disorder (DID)

A complex dissociative disorder characterized by the presence of two or more distinct personality states or identities that recurrently take control of the individual's behavior. DID is strongly associated with severe and sustained childhood trauma.

Doom Scrolling

The habit of continuously scrolling through negative or distressing news and social media content, often late at night or during periods of stress. Doom scrolling can increase anxiety, disrupt sleep, amplify feelings of helplessness, and contribute to emotional exhaustion. It is often driven by the brain's threat-detection system seeking information about potential dangers, combined with the design of social media platforms that reward continuous engagement.

Dopamine

A neurotransmitter that plays a central role in motivation, reward, pleasure, attention, and movement. Dopamine is involved in the brain's reward circuitry and is implicated in conditions such as ADHD, depression, addiction, and schizophrenia. In popular culture, terms like "dopamine detox" and "dopamine hit" have become widespread, though the neuroscience is often oversimplified. Clinically, understanding dopamine helps explain why certain behaviors become compulsive and why motivation can feel impaired in various mental health conditions.

DSM-5-TR

The Diagnostic and Statistical Manual of Mental Disorders, Fifth Edition, Text Revision, published by the American Psychiatric Association. It is the standard classification system used by mental health professionals in the United States for the diagnosis of mental health conditions.

Dysthymia (Persistent Depressive Disorder)

A chronic form of depression lasting at least two years in adults. While the symptoms may be less intense than major depressive disorder, their persistent nature can significantly impair daily functioning and quality of life.

ECT (Electroconvulsive Therapy)

A medical procedure in which controlled electrical currents are passed through the brain to induce a brief seizure, used to treat severe depression, treatment-resistant conditions, catatonia, and certain acute psychiatric emergencies. Modern ECT is performed under general anesthesia with muscle relaxants.

EMDR (Eye Movement Desensitization and Reprocessing)

An evidence-based psychotherapy technique used primarily for the treatment of trauma and PTSD. EMDR involves processing traumatic memories while engaging in bilateral stimulation, typically through guided eye movements, to reduce the emotional intensity of disturbing memories.

Emotional Dysregulation

The inability to effectively manage and respond to emotional experiences. It is characterized by intense emotional reactions, mood swings, and difficulty returning to a baseline emotional state. Emotional dysregulation is a central feature of borderline personality disorder, ADHD, and trauma-related conditions.

Emotional Flooding

A state in which a person becomes so overwhelmed by emotion that their capacity for rational thought, communication, and problem-solving is significantly impaired. During emotional flooding, the nervous system enters a heightened stress response, making it difficult to listen, stay calm, or respond constructively.

Emotional flooding is commonly discussed in couples therapy and is a key concept in the Gottman Method. Learning to recognize and manage flooding is essential for healthy conflict resolution.

Emotional Intelligence

The capacity to recognize, understand, manage, and effectively express one's own emotions, as well as to recognize and respond appropriately to the emotions of others. Higher emotional intelligence is associated with better mental health outcomes and interpersonal relationships.

Enabling

Behavior by family members, friends, or others that inadvertently supports or perpetuates a person's dysfunctional patterns, such as substance abuse or avoidance. Enabling often stems from a desire to help but ultimately prevents the individual from experiencing the natural consequences of their behavior.

Enmeshment

A relational pattern in which personal boundaries between individuals, often family members, become blurred or nonexistent. In enmeshed relationships, one person's emotions, identity, and needs become entangled with another's, making it difficult to distinguish where one person ends and the other begins. Enmeshment can interfere with the development of a healthy sense of self and is frequently addressed in family therapy, recovery from codependency, and treatment of personality disorders.

ERP (Exposure and Response Prevention)

A specialized form of cognitive behavioral therapy considered the gold-standard treatment for obsessive-compulsive disorder. ERP involves gradually exposing the individual to anxiety-provoking thoughts or situations while preventing the compulsive response. Over time, this process reduces the power of obsessions and breaks the OCD cycle.

Executive Functioning

A set of cognitive processes that include working memory, flexible thinking, and self-control. Executive functions are essential for planning, organizing, initiating tasks, managing time, and regulating emotions. Deficits in executive functioning are commonly associated with ADHD, traumatic brain injury, and certain mood disorders.

Family Therapy

A form of psychotherapy that addresses the mental health of the family unit as a system. It focuses on improving communication, resolving conflicts, and understanding how family dynamics contribute to individual members' psychological difficulties.

Fawn Response

A trauma response characterized by people-pleasing, over-accommodating, and prioritizing others' needs at the expense of one's own in order to avoid conflict, rejection, or danger. The fawn response is sometimes described as the fourth survival response alongside fight, flight, and freeze. It is commonly associated with complex trauma, childhood emotional neglect, and environments where safety depended on keeping others calm or satisfied. Recognizing the fawn response is an important step in trauma recovery and boundary work.

Flat Affect

A significant reduction in the range and intensity of emotional expression. The person's face may appear immobile and unresponsive, voice tone may be monotonous, and eye contact may be poor. Flat affect is commonly associated with schizophrenia.

Flight of Ideas

A thought disorder characterized by a nearly continuous flow of rapid speech with abrupt changes from topic to topic, typically based on understandable associations. It is commonly observed during manic episodes in bipolar disorder.

GAD (Generalized Anxiety Disorder)

A chronic anxiety disorder characterized by excessive, uncontrollable worry about a wide range of everyday concerns such as health, finances, work, and family. Physical symptoms often include muscle tension, restlessness, fatigue, difficulty concentrating, and sleep disturbances.

Gaslighting

A form of psychological manipulation in which one person causes another to question their own reality, memory, or perception. Over time, gaslighting can erode the victim's self-confidence and mental health. It is commonly associated with abusive relationships.

Grief

The natural emotional response to loss, particularly the death of a loved one. Grief can manifest as sadness, anger, guilt, yearning, and physical symptoms. While grief is a normal process, prolonged or complicated grief may require professional support.

Grounding Techniques

Strategies used to bring a person's awareness back to the present moment during episodes of anxiety, dissociation, panic, or emotional overwhelm. Common grounding techniques include the 5-4-3-2-1 sensory exercise (naming things you can see, hear, touch, smell, and taste), deep breathing, holding a cold object, pressing feet into the floor, and describing your surroundings aloud. Grounding is widely used in trauma therapy, crisis intervention, and everyday stress management.

Group Therapy

A form of psychotherapy in which a trained therapist leads sessions with multiple participants who share similar concerns. Group therapy provides peer support, diverse perspectives, and opportunities to practice interpersonal skills in a safe environment.

Hallucination

A sensory perception that occurs without an external stimulus. Hallucinations can be auditory, visual, tactile, olfactory, or gustatory. Auditory hallucinations, such as hearing voices, are most commonly associated with schizophrenia, but hallucinations can also occur in other conditions and during substance use.

Harm Reduction

An approach to substance use and other risky behaviors that prioritizes reducing negative consequences rather than demanding immediate abstinence. Harm reduction strategies meet individuals where they are and include education, clean supply programs, and supervised consumption sites.

Hypersomnia

A condition characterized by excessive daytime sleepiness or prolonged nighttime sleep despite adequate rest. It can be a symptom of depression, certain medical conditions, or a standalone sleep disorder.

Hypervigilance

A state of heightened alertness and constant scanning for potential threats, even in objectively safe environments. Hypervigilance is a hallmark symptom of PTSD, complex trauma, and anxiety disorders. It can manifest as difficulty relaxing, startling easily, trouble sleeping, and interpreting neutral situations as dangerous. While hypervigilance often developed as a protective response to real danger, it can become exhausting and disabling when the nervous system remains stuck in threat-detection mode.

Hypomania

A mood state characterized by elevated energy, decreased need for sleep, increased activity, and sometimes irritability or impulsive behavior that is less severe than full mania. Hypomania is a defining feature of Bipolar II disorder and does not typically include psychotic features.

IFS (Internal Family Systems)

A psychotherapy model that views the mind as naturally composed of multiple sub-personalities or "parts," each with its own perspective and qualities. IFS helps individuals identify and understand protective and wounded parts of themselves, access a core "Self" characterized by curiosity and compassion, and heal internal conflicts. It is widely used for trauma, anxiety, depression, and relationship issues.

Informed Consent

The process by which a patient is provided with clear, understandable information about a proposed treatment, including its risks, benefits, alternatives, and the right to refuse. Informed consent is a legal and ethical requirement in all mental health treatment settings.

Inner Child Work

A therapeutic approach that involves connecting with and healing the emotional wounds, unmet needs, and beliefs formed during childhood. Inner child work recognizes that many adult patterns, such as people-pleasing, fear of abandonment, self-sabotage, and difficulty trusting, originate from childhood experiences of neglect, criticism, instability, or trauma. Techniques may include visualization, journaling, letter writing, and guided dialogue with the younger self. It is used across multiple therapy models including IFS, psychodynamic therapy, and schema therapy.

Insomnia

A sleep disorder characterized by persistent difficulty falling asleep, staying asleep, or waking too early and being unable to return to sleep. Chronic insomnia significantly impacts mood, cognitive function, physical health, and overall quality of life.

Interpersonal Therapy (IPT)

A structured, time-limited psychotherapy that focuses on improving interpersonal relationships and social functioning to reduce symptoms of depression and other mood disorders. IPT addresses four key areas: grief, role disputes, role transitions, and interpersonal deficits. It is one of the most well-researched treatments for major depressive disorder.

Intrusive Thoughts

Unwanted, involuntary thoughts, images, or impulses that are often disturbing or distressing. Intrusive thoughts are a core feature of OCD, but they can also occur in anxiety disorders, PTSD, depression, and in the general population. Having intrusive thoughts does not indicate intent or desire to act on them.

Glossary: J – R

Ketamine-Assisted Therapy

The clinical use of ketamine or its derivative esketamine (Spravato) to treat severe depression, treatment-resistant depression, suicidal ideation, and certain anxiety and PTSD symptoms. Unlike traditional antidepressants that target serotonin, ketamine acts on the glutamate system and can produce rapid relief, sometimes within hours. Treatment is administered under medical supervision, typically via IV infusion, intramuscular injection, or FDA-approved nasal spray. Ketamine-assisted therapy represents a significant shift toward rapid-acting interventions in psychiatric care.

Labile Mood

Rapid, unpredictable, and often exaggerated shifts in mood or emotional expression. Mood lability can occur in bipolar disorder, borderline personality disorder, neurological conditions, and certain medication reactions.

Learned Helplessness

A psychological state in which a person who has repeatedly experienced uncontrollable negative events comes to believe they are powerless to change their circumstances. This concept is central to certain theories of depression and trauma.

LGBTQ+ Mental Health

The specialized consideration of mental health challenges faced by lesbian, gay, bisexual, transgender, queer, and other gender and sexual minority individuals. LGBTQ+ individuals face elevated rates of depression, anxiety, and suicidality, often linked to minority stress, discrimination, and lack of affirming care.

Major Depressive Disorder (MDD)

A mood disorder characterized by persistent feelings of sadness, hopelessness, loss of interest in activities, changes in appetite and sleep, fatigue, difficulty concentrating, and in severe cases, thoughts of death or suicide. MDD is one of the most common mental health conditions worldwide.

Mania

An abnormally elevated, expansive, or irritable mood state lasting at least seven days and characterized by increased energy, reduced need for sleep, grandiosity, pressured speech, racing thoughts, distractibility, and impulsive behavior. Mania is a hallmark of Bipolar I disorder and may include psychotic features.

MAT (Medication-Assisted Treatment)

The use of FDA-approved medications, in combination with counseling and behavioral therapies, to treat substance use disorders. MAT is considered the gold standard for opioid use disorder treatment and includes medications such as buprenorphine, methadone, and naltrexone.

Measurement-Based Care

An approach to mental health treatment that uses standardized assessment tools and regular symptom tracking to guide clinical decisions. Rather than relying solely on subjective impressions, measurement-based care provides objective data on how a patient is responding to treatment over time. This allows clinicians to adjust medications, therapy approaches, or treatment intensity based on measurable progress. It is increasingly considered a best practice in psychiatric care.

Medication Management

The ongoing process of monitoring and adjusting psychiatric medications to achieve optimal therapeutic effect while minimizing side effects. Effective medication management involves regular follow-up appointments, dosage adjustments, and coordination between providers and patients.

Mental Health Stigma

The negative attitudes, beliefs, stereotypes, and discriminatory behaviors directed toward individuals with mental health conditions. Stigma is one of the most significant barriers to seeking and receiving mental health treatment.

Mindfulness

The practice of paying attention to the present moment with intention and without judgment. Mindfulness-based interventions have demonstrated effectiveness for reducing stress, managing chronic pain, preventing relapse in depression, and improving overall emotional well-being.

Mood Disorder

A category of mental health conditions primarily characterized by disturbances in a person's emotional state. Major mood disorders include major depressive disorder, bipolar disorder, persistent depressive disorder, and cyclothymic disorder.

Mood Stabilizer

A class of psychiatric medications used to treat mood swings, particularly the highs and lows associated with bipolar disorder. Common mood stabilizers include lithium, valproic acid, lamotrigine, and carbamazepine.

Narcissistic Personality Disorder (NPD)

A personality disorder characterized by a pervasive pattern of grandiosity, need for admiration, and lack of empathy. Individuals with NPD often have fragile self-esteem masked by an outward appearance of confidence and superiority.

Nervous System Regulation

The process of helping the autonomic nervous system move from states of heightened stress (fight, flight, or freeze) back to a calm, connected baseline. Regulation can occur through self-regulation practices such as deep breathing, movement, and mindfulness, or through co-regulation with another safe, calm person. Nervous system regulation has become one of the most widely discussed concepts in modern mental health, particularly in trauma-informed care and body-based therapies. It is grounded in the understanding that many mental health symptoms reflect a nervous system that has become stuck in survival mode.

Neuroception

A term coined by Dr. Stephen Porges to describe the nervous system's subconscious process of continuously scanning the environment for cues of safety, danger, or life threat. Unlike conscious perception, neuroception operates below awareness and influences the body's automatic responses, such as feeling tense in a seemingly safe room or relaxing in the presence of a trusted person. Understanding neuroception helps explain why people with trauma histories may react to situations that appear objectively safe, and why certain environments, tones of voice, or body language can trigger defensive responses without conscious thought.

Neurodivergent

A term used to describe individuals whose neurological development and functioning differ from what is considered typical. Neurodivergent conditions include ADHD, autism spectrum disorder, dyslexia, and Tourette syndrome, among others.

Neurofeedback

A form of biofeedback that trains the brain to regulate its own electrical activity by providing real-time feedback on brainwave patterns. During a session, sensors placed on the scalp measure brain activity while the individual engages in activities that reward desired brainwave states. Neurofeedback is used as a complementary treatment for ADHD, anxiety, depression, PTSD, insomnia, and traumatic brain injury. While research continues to develop, many clinicians report positive results when neurofeedback is combined with other therapeutic approaches.

Neuroplasticity

The brain's ability to reorganize itself by forming new neural connections throughout life in response to experience, learning, injury, and therapeutic intervention. Neuroplasticity is the biological basis for why therapy, mindfulness practices, and behavioral changes can produce lasting improvements in mental health. It counters the outdated belief that the brain is fixed after a certain age and provides scientific hope that recovery, growth, and change remain possible across the lifespan.

Neurotransmitter

Chemical messengers in the brain that transmit signals between nerve cells. Key neurotransmitters involved in mental health include serotonin, dopamine, norepinephrine, GABA, and glutamate. Imbalances in neurotransmitter activity are implicated in various psychiatric conditions.

OCD (Obsessive-Compulsive Disorder)

A chronic mental health condition characterized by recurring, unwanted thoughts, images, or urges (obsessions) and repetitive behaviors or mental acts (compulsions) performed to reduce the anxiety caused by the obsessions. Common themes include contamination, harm, symmetry, and forbidden thoughts.

Oppositional Defiant Disorder (ODD)

A childhood behavioral disorder characterized by a pattern of angry, irritable mood, argumentative and defiant behavior, and vindictiveness toward authority figures. ODD is more severe than typical childhood defiance and significantly impairs social and academic functioning.

Panic Attack

A sudden episode of intense fear or discomfort that reaches a peak within minutes and includes physical symptoms such as heart palpitations, sweating, trembling, shortness of breath, chest pain, dizziness, and feelings of unreality or impending doom. Panic attacks can occur unexpectedly or in response to a specific trigger.

Panic Disorder

An anxiety disorder characterized by recurrent, unexpected panic attacks accompanied by persistent worry about future attacks or significant behavioral changes to avoid them. Panic disorder often co-occurs with agoraphobia.

Paranoia

An unfounded or exaggerated distrust and suspicion of others. Paranoia ranges in severity from common, mild suspicious thinking to the fixed paranoid delusions seen in psychotic disorders. It can also occur in the context of anxiety, trauma, or substance use.

Parts Work

A therapeutic framework that understands the mind as containing multiple sub-personalities or "parts," each carrying its own emotions, beliefs, and protective roles. In parts work, symptoms like anxiety, anger, self-sabotage, or numbing are understood as parts trying to protect the individual from emotional pain. The most well-known parts-based model is Internal Family Systems (IFS), but the concept appears across several therapeutic approaches. The goal is not to eliminate parts but to understand their protective intent and help them release burdens carried from past experiences.

People-Pleasing

A behavioral pattern characterized by habitually prioritizing others' needs, feelings, and approval over one's own, often at the cost of personal well-being, authenticity, and boundary maintenance. People-pleasing frequently develops as a survival strategy in childhood environments where love, safety, or acceptance felt conditional on keeping others happy. While often praised socially, chronic people-pleasing can lead to burnout, resentment, identity confusion, and difficulty recognizing one's own needs. It is closely related to the fawn response and is commonly addressed in therapy for codependency, trauma, and self-worth.

Personality Disorder

A group of mental health conditions characterized by enduring, inflexible patterns of thinking, feeling, and behaving that deviate significantly from cultural expectations, cause distress, and impair functioning. The DSM-5 identifies ten specific personality disorders organized into three clusters.

Pharmacotherapy

The treatment of mental health disorders through the use of medications. Pharmacotherapy is often combined with psychotherapy for a comprehensive approach to treatment and requires careful monitoring for effectiveness and side effects.

Phobia

An excessive and irrational fear response to a specific object, situation, or activity that poses little or no actual danger. Specific phobias are among the most common anxiety disorders and include fears of animals, heights, flying, blood, and enclosed spaces.

Polyvagal Theory

A neurophysiological framework developed by Dr. Stephen Porges that describes how the autonomic nervous system operates through three primary states: ventral vagal (safe, social, connected), sympathetic (fight or flight), and dorsal vagal (shutdown, freeze, collapse). Polyvagal theory explains that the nervous system constantly scans for safety and danger through a process called neuroception, and that many trauma symptoms, anxiety responses, and relational difficulties can be understood as the body's automatic survival strategies. While some of its biological claims are debated in the scientific community, the framework has been widely adopted in trauma therapy and has given millions of people language for understanding their own nervous system responses.

Positive Psychology

A branch of psychology that focuses on strengths, virtues, and factors that contribute to human flourishing rather than solely treating pathology. Positive psychology interventions include gratitude practices, strength identification, and fostering positive relationships.

Prodrome

An early set of signs or symptoms that may indicate the onset of a mental health condition before full diagnostic criteria are met. Recognizing prodromal symptoms is particularly important in conditions like schizophrenia, where early intervention can improve outcomes.

Prognosis

A prediction or estimate of the likely course and outcome of a disorder based on clinical knowledge, research evidence, and the individual's specific circumstances. In mental health, prognosis is influenced by factors such as early treatment, support systems, comorbidities, and adherence to treatment.

Psychedelic-Assisted Therapy

An emerging therapeutic approach that uses psychedelic substances, such as psilocybin, MDMA, or ketamine, in combination with structured psychotherapy to treat conditions including treatment-resistant depression, PTSD, anxiety, and addiction. These substances are believed to promote neuroplasticity, reduce default-mode network rigidity, and facilitate emotional processing. As of 2026, ketamine is the only psychedelic legally available for clinical use nationwide in the United States, while psilocybin and MDMA are in advanced clinical trials and state-level pilot programs. All psychedelic-assisted therapy should be conducted under professional medical supervision.

Psychiatric Evaluation

A comprehensive clinical assessment conducted by a psychiatric provider to determine the nature and extent of a person's mental health concerns. It typically includes a clinical interview, mental status examination, review of medical and psychiatric history, and development of a treatment plan.

Psychiatric Nurse Practitioner (PMHNP)

An advanced practice registered nurse with specialized training in psychiatric and mental health care. PMHNPs are board-certified to diagnose mental health conditions, prescribe medications, provide psychotherapy, and develop comprehensive treatment plans across the lifespan.

Psychiatrist

A medical doctor who specializes in the diagnosis, treatment, and prevention of mental health disorders. Psychiatrists are licensed to prescribe medications and may also provide psychotherapy.

Psychoanalysis

A therapeutic approach developed by Sigmund Freud that explores unconscious thoughts, early life experiences, and repressed memories to understand and resolve psychological distress. While classical psychoanalysis is less common today, its concepts have influenced many modern therapeutic approaches.

Psychodynamic Therapy

A form of psychotherapy rooted in psychoanalytic principles that focuses on how unconscious processes, early life experiences, and recurring relational patterns influence current emotions and behavior. Unlike classical psychoanalysis, psychodynamic therapy is typically shorter in duration and more conversational. It is effective for depression, anxiety, personality disorders, and chronic relational difficulties.

Psychoeducation

The process of providing patients and their families with information about mental health conditions, treatment options, coping strategies, and self-management techniques. Psychoeducation is a fundamental component of effective mental health treatment.

Psychomotor Agitation

A state of restless, purposeless physical activity driven by mental tension. Examples include pacing, hand-wringing, fidgeting, and an inability to sit still. It is commonly seen in anxiety disorders, major depression, bipolar mania, and psychotic disorders.

Psychomotor Retardation

A slowing of physical movement and mental

processing. It may manifest as slowed speech, delayed responses, reduced body movements, and difficulty initiating tasks. Psychomotor retardation is commonly associated with severe depression.

Psychosis

A mental state characterized by a disconnection from reality, typically involving hallucinations, delusions, and disorganized thinking. Psychosis can occur in the context of schizophrenia, bipolar disorder, severe depression, substance use, medical conditions, and extreme stress.

Psychotherapy

The treatment of mental health conditions through structured conversation and interaction with a trained mental health professional. Also known as talk therapy, psychotherapy encompasses many approaches including CBT, DBT, psychodynamic therapy, and interpersonal therapy.

PTSD (Post-Traumatic Stress Disorder)

A mental health condition that develops in some individuals after experiencing or witnessing a terrifying or life-threatening event. Symptoms include intrusive re-experiencing of the event, avoidance of reminders, negative changes in thinking and mood, and hyperarousal.

Rapport

The trusting, harmonious relationship between a patient and their mental health provider. Strong therapeutic rapport is one of the most significant predictors of positive treatment outcomes across all forms of psychotherapy.

Recovery

In mental health, recovery refers to the ongoing process of managing one's condition and working toward a fulfilling, meaningful life. Recovery is individualized and may involve treatment, peer support, self-management strategies, and personal growth, regardless of whether symptoms fully resolve.

Relapse

The return of symptoms after a period of improvement or remission. Relapse is a common part of many mental health and substance use disorders and should be viewed as a signal to revisit and adjust the treatment plan rather than as a failure.

Reparenting

A therapeutic concept in which an individual learns to provide for themselves the emotional care, validation, stability, and nurturing they did not adequately receive in childhood. Reparenting may involve developing a compassionate inner voice, establishing consistent self-care routines, setting boundaries, and learning to comfort oneself during distress, skills that a secure caregiver would have modeled. It is central to inner child work, schema therapy, and recovery from childhood emotional neglect.

Resilience

The ability to adapt, recover, and grow in the face of adversity, trauma, or significant stress. Resilience is not a fixed trait but a set of skills and perspectives that can be developed and strengthened through supportive relationships, coping strategies, and professional guidance.

Rumination

A pattern of repetitive, passive thinking about the causes, consequences, and symptoms of distress without taking action to address them. Rumination is closely linked to the onset and maintenance of depression and anxiety.

Glossary: S - Z

Schizoaffective Disorder

A chronic mental health condition that includes symptoms of both schizophrenia, such as hallucinations or delusions, and a mood disorder, such as depression or mania. It requires simultaneous treatment of both psychotic and mood symptoms.

Schizophrenia

A severe, chronic mental health disorder characterized by distortions in thinking, perception, emotions, language, sense of self, and behavior. Core symptoms include hallucinations, delusions, disorganized speech, reduced emotional expression, and difficulty with cognitive tasks.

Seasonal Affective Disorder (SAD)

A type of depression that follows a seasonal pattern, most commonly occurring during the fall and winter months when daylight hours are shortest. Treatment may include light therapy, psychotherapy, and medication.

Self-Care

The deliberate practice of activities that maintain and improve physical, mental, and emotional health. Self-care strategies include adequate sleep, nutrition, exercise, social connection, relaxation techniques, setting boundaries, and engaging in meaningful activities.

Self-Compassion

The practice of treating oneself with the same kindness, understanding, and patience that one would offer a close friend during times of suffering or failure. Self-compassion has been shown to reduce anxiety, depression, and self-criticism while increasing emotional resilience.

Self-Esteem

An individual's overall subjective evaluation of their own worth and value. Low self-esteem is associated with depression, anxiety, relationship difficulties, and vulnerability to substance use, while healthy self-esteem contributes to emotional well-being and resilience.

Self-Harm

The deliberate injury of one's own body, typically as a way to cope with emotional pain, intense anger, or frustration. Common forms include cutting, burning, and hitting. Self-harm is not the same as a suicide attempt, though individuals who self-harm are at increased risk for suicidal behavior. Professional help is strongly recommended.

Self-Regulation

The ability to manage one's own emotional, physiological, and behavioral responses to stress, distress, or overstimulation. Self-regulation involves recognizing internal states, using coping strategies to return to a calm baseline, and making conscious choices rather than reacting impulsively. It is a foundational skill in emotional intelligence, trauma recovery, and healthy relationships. Common self-regulation tools include deep breathing, movement, mindfulness, journaling, and sensory grounding.

Sleep Hygiene

A set of behavioral and environmental practices designed to promote consistent, restorative sleep. Good sleep hygiene includes maintaining a regular sleep schedule, creating a comfortable sleep environment, limiting screen time before bed, and avoiding caffeine and alcohol close to bedtime.

Social Anxiety Disorder

An anxiety disorder characterized by significant

fear of social situations in which a person may be scrutinized, judged, or embarrassed. The fear is disproportionate to the actual threat and often leads to avoidance of social interactions, work settings, or performance situations.

Somatic Symptom Disorder

A condition in which a person experiences physical symptoms, such as pain, fatigue, or gastrointestinal distress, that are accompanied by excessive thoughts, feelings, or behaviors related to those symptoms. The distress is real and significant, regardless of whether a medical cause is identified.

Somatic Therapy

A body-centered therapeutic approach that addresses the connection between the mind and body in processing trauma, stress, and emotional pain. Techniques may include breathwork, body awareness, movement, and touch-based interventions. Somatic therapy is based on the understanding that traumatic experiences can become stored in the body and that healing often requires engagement with physical sensations, not only cognitive processing.

Spravato (Esketamine)

An FDA-approved nasal spray derived from ketamine, used for the treatment of treatment-resistant depression and major depressive disorder with suicidal ideation in adults. Spravato acts on the glutamate system and can produce noticeable symptom relief within hours to days, unlike traditional antidepressants which may take weeks. It must be administered under medical supervision in a certified healthcare setting due to potential side effects including dissociation, sedation, and elevated blood pressure. Patients are monitored for at least two hours after each dose.

Substance Use Disorder (SUD)

A medical condition characterized by the compulsive use of substances despite harmful consequences. SUD involves changes in brain chemistry that affect judgment, decision-making, memory, and behavior. Treatment typically combines medication, counseling, and support services.

Suicidal Ideation

Thoughts about, considerations of, or planning for ending one's own life. Suicidal ideation ranges from passive wishes to die to active planning. Any expression of suicidal ideation should be taken seriously, and immediate professional help should be sought. If you or someone you know is in crisis, please contact the 988 Suicide and Crisis Lifeline by calling or texting 988.

Tardive Dyskinesia

A movement disorder characterized by involuntary, repetitive movements, particularly of the face, tongue, and jaw. It can develop as a side effect of long-term use of certain antipsychotic medications and may be partially or fully irreversible.

Therapeutic Alliance

The collaborative, trusting bond between a patient and their mental health provider that is characterized by agreement on treatment goals, the tasks of therapy, and an emotional bond. Research consistently shows that a strong therapeutic alliance is one of the best predictors of positive treatment outcomes.

Therapy Intensives

Concentrated therapeutic experiences designed to replicate the benefits of months of traditional therapy in a shorter timeframe, typically ranging from a few hours to several days. Rather than weekly sessions spread across months, intensives provide an extended, immersive block of therapeutic work. They are increasingly used for EMDR, trauma processing, couples therapy, and OCD treatment. Therapy intensives are gaining popularity among clients experiencing burnout who seek faster relief and among those whose schedules make weekly appointments difficult.

Thought Disorder

A disruption in the organization and flow of thoughts that affects a person's ability to communicate coherently. Types include tangential thinking, loose associations, word salad, and thought blocking. Thought disorders are most commonly associated with psychotic conditions.

Tic Disorder

A condition characterized by sudden, repetitive, involuntary movements or vocalizations called tics. Tourette syndrome is the most well-known tic disorder and involves both motor and vocal tics persisting for more than one year.

Toxic Positivity

The excessive and rigid insistence on maintaining a positive mindset regardless of circumstances, often dismissing, minimizing, or suppressing genuine emotional experiences such as sadness, anger, grief, or frustration. Toxic positivity can invalidate a person's real struggles and create pressure to appear fine when they are not. Common examples include telling someone who is grieving to "look on the bright side" or insisting that "everything happens for a reason." Healthy emotional processing requires space for both positive and difficult feelings.

Transference

The unconscious redirection of feelings about one person, often a parent or significant figure, onto the therapist or another person in the present. Understanding transference is an important element in psychodynamic and psychoanalytic therapies.

Trauma

A deeply distressing or disturbing experience that overwhelms an individual's ability to cope. Trauma can result from a single event, such as an accident or assault, or from sustained exposure to harmful conditions, such as childhood abuse or domestic violence. The effects of trauma can be far-reaching and long-lasting.

Trauma Bonding

A strong emotional attachment that forms between a person and their abuser, driven by cycles of intermittent reinforcement, alternating between abuse or neglect and moments of kindness, affection, or relief. Trauma bonds help explain why individuals in abusive relationships often struggle to leave, return to their abuser, or defend the relationship despite clear harm. The bond is not a sign of weakness; it is a predictable neurobiological response to inconsistent reward and punishment. Understanding trauma bonding is essential in domestic violence recovery, therapy for abuse survivors, and clinical work with attachment wounds.

Trauma-Focused CBT (TF-CBT)

An evidence-based psychotherapy model designed specifically for children and adolescents who have experienced significant trauma. TF-CBT combines trauma-sensitive interventions with cognitive behavioral principles and includes a strong parent or caregiver component. It addresses trauma-related symptoms such as PTSD, depression, anxiety, and behavioral difficulties.

Trauma-Informed Care

An approach to treatment that recognizes the widespread impact of trauma and integrates this understanding into all aspects of service delivery. Trauma-informed care emphasizes physical, psychological, and emotional safety, trustworthiness, peer support, collaboration, and cultural sensitivity.

Treatment-Resistant Depression

Depression that does not adequately respond to at least two different antidepressant medications given at adequate doses for adequate durations. Treatment options for resistant depression may include medication augmentation strategies, ECT, ketamine or esketamine therapy, TMS, and specialized psychotherapy.

Trichotillomania

A body-focused repetitive behavior disorder characterized by the recurrent, compulsive pulling out of one's own hair, resulting in hair loss and significant distress. It is classified among obsessive-compulsive and related disorders.

Trigger

A stimulus, such as a sound, smell, image, word, or situation, that evokes a strong emotional or psychological response, often related to past traumatic experiences. Identifying personal triggers is an important component of managing conditions such as PTSD, anxiety, and substance use disorders.

Vagus Nerve

The longest cranial nerve in the body, running from the brainstem through the neck, chest, and abdomen. The vagus nerve plays a critical role in regulating heart rate, digestion, breathing, and the body's stress response. It is the primary nerve of the parasympathetic nervous system and is central to polyvagal theory. Stimulating the vagus nerve through practices such as deep diaphragmatic breathing, humming, cold water exposure, and gentle movement can promote a sense of calm and help shift the body out of a fight-or-flight state. Vagus nerve stimulation has also been developed as a medical device treatment for epilepsy and treatment-resistant depression.

Virtual Reality (VR) Therapy

The use of immersive virtual reality technology as a therapeutic tool in mental health treatment. VR therapy allows individuals to experience controlled, realistic simulations of anxiety-provoking situations, such as heights, social settings, or trauma-related environments, within the safety of a clinical setting. It is increasingly used for exposure therapy in phobias, PTSD, social anxiety, and pain management. As VR technology becomes more accessible, it is emerging as a versatile complement to traditional therapy approaches.

Window of Tolerance

A concept developed by Dr. Daniel Siegel that describes the optimal zone of nervous system arousal in which a person can function effectively, process emotions, think clearly, and respond to stress without becoming overwhelmed. When a person moves above their window of tolerance, they may experience hyperarousal, anxiety, panic, rage, or hypervigilance. When they drop below it, they may experience hypoarousal, numbness, shutdown, disconnection, or depression. Trauma, chronic stress, and adverse childhood experiences can narrow the window of tolerance, while therapy, grounding practices, and co-regulation can help widen it over time.

Withdrawal

The physical and psychological symptoms that occur when a person reduces or stops using a substance to which they have become dependent. Withdrawal symptoms vary by substance and can range from mild anxiety and irritability to life-threatening seizures and delirium. Medical supervision is recommended for withdrawal from alcohol, benzodiazepines, and opioids.

Part Two: Case Studies

Recognizing Mental Health Conditions

The following case studies are fictional composites created for educational purposes. They illustrate how common mental health conditions appear in daily life, both for the person experiencing them and for the people around them. Each entry follows a consistent format for easy reference.

How to use this section: Topics are arranged alphabetically. Each opens with a brief overview, followed by case snapshots, and closes with practical tips for individuals and loved ones.

Acute Stress During Life Transitions

Major life changes, even positive ones, can create grief, identity disruption, and nervous system overload. The person is not necessarily mentally ill; they may be emotionally overextended while adapting.

Stephanie, 50

What she experiences: After leaving a 25-year career, Stephanie feels unsettled despite having wanted the change. She second-guesses herself constantly, lies awake at night, cries unexpectedly, and wonders why she is struggling when others call her move "brave."

What loved ones notice: Her partner sees her restless, irritable, and emotionally fragile. Friends say "give it time," which makes Stephanie feel more alone because it fails to acknowledge how destabilizing transitions can be.

Helpful Tips

For Individuals: Managing the Internal Shift

Normalize Emotional Intensity: It is common to feel a sense of "identity disruption." When you leave a long-term role or environment, you aren't just changing your schedule; you are changing how you define yourself. Recognizing that it is normal to feel "unsettled" or even to "cry unexpectedly" helps reduce the secondary shame of struggling with a positive move.

Maintain Biological Anchors: Stress often disrupts our basic biology. By intentionally maintaining routines for **sleep, meals, and movement**, you provide your nervous system with "predictability anchors." This signals to your brain that despite the external chaos, your immediate environment is still safe and structured.

Balance the Narrative: Transitions involve a "dual-process" of mourning what was left behind (the loss) and looking toward the future (the opportunity). If you only focus on the opportunity, you suppress grief; if you only focus on the loss, you may stall. Talking openly about both allows for a more integrated and healthy adjustment.

External Support: Short-term therapy or coaching provides a neutral space to process these shifts. A professional can help you distinguish between a temporary adjustment reaction and a deeper clinical issue, offering tools to manage the "nervous system overload" that often accompanies new beginnings.

For Loved Ones: Providing a Steady Foundation

Validate the Instability: The most helpful thing a loved one can do is acknowledge that **change is destabilizing**. Rather than trying to "fix" the person's mood, simply affirming that their feelings make sense given the scale of the change can lower their anxiety significantly.

Avoid Toxic Positivity: Phrases like "you should be grateful" or "you're so brave" can be unintentionally minimizing. These comments often make the individual feel they have to hide their struggle to meet your expectations. It's better to acknowledge the difficulty than to push for a positive outlook.

Practical Support vs. Emotional Steadiness: * **Practical Support:** Help with the "mental load", handling chores, meals, or logistics, so the individual has more bandwidth to process the transition.

Emotional Steadiness: Be the "calm in the storm." If you remain grounded and patient, you provide a safe harbor for them to be "irritable" or "fragile" without the fear that their temporary state will ruin the relationship.

ADHD

ADHD is a neurodevelopmental difference affecting executive function, not a lack of intelligence or motivation. Adults with ADHD often struggle with organization, time management, follow-through, and sustaining attention on low-interest tasks, while excelling at creative or high-engagement work.

Olivia, 35

What she experiences: Olivia starts mornings with good intentions but becomes distracted by emails, new ideas, and half-finished tasks. Time feels slippery. She procrastinates paperwork, interrupts without meaning to, and feels constant shame from falling short of expectations she knows she can meet.

What loved ones notice: Coworkers see her as energetic but disorganized. Her romantic partners become frustrated by unfinished chores and forgetfulness, often interpreting it as carelessness, not seeing how hard she is working internally to compensate.

Marcus, 35

What he experiences: Marcus, a developer, starts dozens of projects but finishes few. He loses his keys daily and struggles with time. His relationship ended because his partner felt he "never listened." He internalizes his executive dysfunction as laziness.

What loved ones notice: His partner felt like a personal assistant rather than a girlfriend. Forgotten dates and unfinished chores created a "parent-child" dynamic that killed intimacy.

Helpful Tips

For Individuals: Building External Scaffolding

External Supports (The "Outsourced" Brain): Since the internal ability to track time and tasks can be inconsistent, you must move that data into the physical world.

Timers and Calendars: These provide a visual or auditory "pulse" to help with time blindness.

Body-Doubling: This is the practice of working alongside another person (physically or virtually). Their quiet presence acts as a social "anchor," making it harder for your mind to drift or for you to succumb to "task paralysis."

Micro-Tasking: The ADHD brain often views a large project (like "Clean the Kitchen") as a single, overwhelming mountain, which triggers avoidance. Breaking it into "Wash three plates" makes the task small enough to bypass the brain's "threat response," allowing you to actually start.

Professional Intervention: Evaluating for **medication or ADHD-informed therapy** is crucial because these challenges are often neurobiological. Medication can help "quiet the noise" or increase dopamine availability, while specialized therapy provides specific workarounds for your unique brain wiring.

The Shame Spiral: Reducing self-blame is perhaps the most important psychological step. When you view a missed deadline as a "symptom of executive dysfunction" rather than a "moral failure" or "laziness," you save the emotional energy needed to solve the problem rather than wasting it on self-criticism.

For Loved Ones: Navigating the "Parent-Child" Trap

The Intentionality Filter: The biggest source of conflict is the belief that the person "doesn't care" because they forgot a chore or an anniversary. Understanding this as **executive function difficulty** (a struggle with the how) rather than **intentional disregard** (a lack of wanting to) changes the conversation from an accusation to a collaboration.

Concrete Communication: Ambiguity is the enemy of executive function. Instead of saying "Could you help out more later?" try "Could you please put the laundry in the dryer at 4:00 PM?" Clear, time-bound, and specific requests are much easier for an ADHD brain to register and execute.

Structure Without Control: There is a thin line between being a supportive partner and becoming a "manager" or "parent."

Support: Asking "What system can we set up so you remember the keys?"

Control: Taking the keys and hanging them up yourself while lecturing them.

The goal is to help the individual build their own external structures so the relationship remains one of two equal adults.

Adults and Social Media

Adults can become emotionally dysregulated by digital environments even when the behavior appears socially normal. Social media may contribute to chronic comparison, attention fragmentation, avoidance of emotional discomfort, and erosion of presence in real relationships.

Monique, 41

What she experiences: Monique opens apps for "a few minutes" and loses half an hour. On hard days, scrolling amplifies self-doubt, everyone else seems more fulfilled. She turns to social media when lonely, but afterward the loneliness remains. Her mind feels trained to seek novelty; quiet moments become hard to tolerate.

What loved ones notice: Her partner sees her reaching for her phone whenever stressed or trying to unwind. During quiet evenings, she is physically present but mentally absent. Friends notice she seems more preoccupied with comparison than she used to be.

Helpful Tips

For Individuals: Restoring Intentionality

Emotional Tracking: Checking in with yourself during and after scrolling is vital because social media often creates a "numbing" effect. By naming the underlying drive, whether it is **connection** (seeking community), **avoidance** (procrastinating on a task), **comparison** (measuring your life against others), or **numbness** (escaping stress), you move the habit from a reflexive impulse to a conscious choice.

Intentional Windows: Setting specific times for use prevents "digital drift," where five minutes turns into an hour. This creates a boundary that protects your focus and prevents the constant dopamine seeking that fragments your attention span.

Active Replacement: Simply trying to "stop scrolling" often fails because it leaves a void. Replacing that time with **walking, conversation, journaling, or rest** provides a different kind of nervous system regulation, one that is grounding and restorative rather than over-stimulating.

For Loved Ones: Shifting from Criticism to Connection

Removing Shame: If a loved one feels judged for their phone use, they are more likely to withdraw further into the device to escape the conflict. Discussing habits without shame allows for an honest conversation about how technology is affecting the relationship without triggering defensiveness.

Monitoring "Presence": The core issue is often not the phone itself, but the loss of **emotional presence**. Acknowledging when someone is physically in the room but mentally absent helps highlight the relational cost of the habit without making it a moral failure.

Collaborative Routines: Rather than acting as a "screen-time police," support healthier habits by offering alternatives. Suggesting a "phone-free walk" or a "tech-free dinner" focuses on the benefit of the shared activity rather than just the restriction of the device. This frames the change as a move toward a more connected life together.

Anxiety

Anxiety involves a brain that has become over-trained to detect threats. The person constantly scans for problems, replays conversations, and struggles to relax, even when nothing is objectively wrong. Physical symptoms such as muscle tension, stomach discomfort, and shallow breathing are common.

Nicole, 33

What she experiences: Nicole wakes with tension already in her body. She mentally reviews yesterday's conversations for mistakes, repeatedly checks emails, and lies awake at night worrying. Coworkers see her as organized; inside, she feels like she is constantly preventing disaster.

What loved ones notice: Her partner sees her seeking reassurance repeatedly, "Are you sure I didn't offend them?", but relief from reassurance never lasts. She rarely appears fully relaxed.

Maria, 34

What she experiences: Maria, a marketing professional, wakes with a tight chest and racing thoughts. She worries about deadlines weeks away, struggles to eat, cancels plans repeatedly, and has lost weight. She believes something is fundamentally wrong with her.

What loved ones notice: Her partner David feels rejected by constant cancellations. He tries reassurance but it has no effect. He has stopped inviting her to events, creating silent distance. He is experiencing caregiver burnout.

Clinical Note

Generalized anxiety disorder develops gradually, making it easy to dismiss as normal stress. Partners often fall into "accommodation" behaviors, taking over responsibilities or giving constant reassurance, which can unintentionally fuel the cycle.

Helpful Tips

For Individuals: Rewiring the Threat Response

Breathing and Grounding: When anxiety peaks, the body's "fight or flight" system takes over. Physical techniques like deep diaphragmatic breathing or grounding exercises (e.g., the 5-4-3-2-1 method), act as a manual override. They signal to the nervous system that the body is safe in the present moment, helping to lower the physical heart rate and muscle tension.

Interrupting Worry Cycles: Anxiety thrives on "repetitive worry," where the mind loops on the same "what-if" scenarios. Learning to identify these loops as they start allows you to set boundaries with your thoughts. Instead of trying to "solve" a worry that has no immediate solution, you practice shifting your attention back to a task or the present environment.

Cognitive Behavioral Therapy (CBT): This is a highly effective, evidence-based approach that focuses on the link between thoughts, feelings, and behaviors. A therapist helps you identify "cognitive distortions" (like catastrophizing or mind-reading) and provides tools to retrain your brain to evaluate threats more realistically.

For Loved Ones: Supporting Without Absorbing

Avoid Emotional Co-Regulation: It is natural to want to "fix" a loved one's distress, but becoming the **sole regulator** of their emotions creates a fragile dynamic. If the anxious person relies entirely on you to feel calm, they don't develop their own internal coping mechanisms. Your role is to be a supportive witness, not the person who "manages" their mood for them.

The Reassurance Trap: One of the most common pitfalls is providing **excessive reassur-**

ance (e.g., "I promise everything will be fine"). While this provides a temporary "hit" of relief, it actually fuels the anxiety cycle by teaching the brain that it needs external validation to feel safe. Instead of reassuring, try validating the feeling: "I can see that you're feeling really overwhelmed right now."

Encouraging Professional Growth: Because anxiety can be exhausting for both parties, encouraging professional help is a sign of care, not a rejection. It ensures the individual gets specialized tools (like CBT or exposure therapy) while you **protect your own boundaries**. Maintaining your own hobbies, social life, and emotional space prevents caregiver burnout and keeps the relationship balanced.

Attachment Wounds

Attachment wounds develop when early caregiving was inconsistent, unpredictable, or emotionally unsafe. As adults, these individuals may become highly sensitive to signs of rejection, misinterpret neutral behavior as withdrawal, and oscillate between seeking closeness and pulling away to protect themselves.

Leah, 36

What she experiences: Leah feels things deeply. A delayed text or cancelled plan can trigger intense fear of abandonment. She replays conversations, scans for evidence of rejection, and either seeks excessive reassurance or withdraws first to avoid being hurt. She wants stable love but struggles to feel safe inside it.

What loved ones notice: Friends and partners experience Leah as caring and intuitive, but notice she reacts strongly to situations they see as minor. Some feel pressure to reassure her constantly. Others feel guilty for needing space.

They sense something tender and fearful underneath her reactions.

Helpful Tips

For Individuals: Moving from Reaction to Reflection

Distinguishing Past from Present: Attachment wounds often cause "emotional flashbacks." When a partner is late or a text goes unanswered, the brain may react as if a core abandonment is happening. Learning to **notice when an old trigger is activating** allows you to separate the historical pain from the current, likely neutral, situation.

The Power of the Pause: Because attachment triggers feel like emergencies, the impulse is often to act immediately (by clinging, protesting, or withdrawing). **Practicing a pause** creates a gap between the feeling and the action, giving the logical brain time to come back online.

Direct Communication: When feeling insecure, people often "act out" their needs through passive-aggression or withdrawal. Shifting to **naming needs directly**, for example, saying "I'm feeling a little anxious, could I have some reassurance?", is a powerful way to build the very security you are seeking.

Attachment-Focused Therapy: Traditional

talk therapy is helpful, but **attachment-focused modalities** specifically target the somatic and relational roots of these wounds. They help "re-parent" the internal sense of self and build a more "earned secure" attachment style.

For Loved Ones: Being a Consistent Anchor

The Importance of Consistency: For someone with attachment wounds, unpredictability is a major trigger. **Responding with consistency**, doing what you say you will do and remaining emotionally steady, helps rebuild their foundational trust in others.

Protecting Vulnerability: It can be easy to lose patience with a partner's high sensitivity, but **avoiding mockery or dismissal** is crucial. What may seem like an overreaction to you is a very real survival response for them. Validating their feelings (even if you don't agree with their logic) prevents further wounding.

Reassurance vs. Over-Regulation: You can **offer reassurance** ("I'm here and I'm not leaving") without becoming the **sole regulator** of their emotions. The goal is to be a supportive partner, not a "security blanket" that prevents them from learning how to soothe themselves.

Clear Boundaries: Maintaining **healthy boundaries** is actually a form of kindness in attachment work. By communicating your own needs and limits clearly and kindly, you model what a healthy, secure relationship looks like and reduce the "guesswork" that often fuels attachment anxiety.

Bipolar Disorder

Bipolar disorder involves alternating episodes of mania (or hypomania) and depression. It is frequently misdiagnosed as depression because patients often seek help only during the lows.

Desiree, 28

What she experiences: Desiree cycles between periods of invincibility, sleeping three hours a night, spending recklessly, and weeks of darkness where she cannot get out of bed. Because people call her "just moody," she delays seeking evaluation.

What loved ones notice: Her best friend Maya never knows which version of Desiree will answer the phone. She feels used during manic phases and abandoned during depressive ones. The unpredictability causes Maya her own emotional distress.

Clinical Note

A thorough history of "highs" is essential for accurate diagnosis. Loved ones often live in "anticipatory dread."

Helpful Tips

For Individuals: Creating Stability Amidst Fluctuation

The Mood Journal (Internal Tracking): Because transitions between mood states can sometimes be subtle at first, keeping a mood journal helps you identify your unique "early warning signs." Tracking sleep, energy, and stressors allows you to notice patterns, such as a decreased need for sleep or increased irritability, before they escalate into a full episode.

Medication Consistency: Bipolar disorder is a biological condition that often requires long-term pharmacological support to stabilize brain chemistry. Taking medication consistently, even when you feel "fine," is the most effective way to prevent relapse and reduce the intensity of future episodes.

The Crisis Plan (Collaborative Safety): Highs and lows can impair judgment, making it difficult to seek help in the moment. Building a crisis plan with your provider while you are stable ensures that there is a clear roadmap for your care. This includes identifying which symptoms require an immediate call to your doctor and who has the authority to help you make safety decisions if you become unable to do so.

For Loved Ones: Balancing Compassion with Firmness

Firm, Compassionate Boundaries: Supporting someone with bipolar disorder requires a delicate balance. Boundaries are not punishments; they are safety rails that protect both the relationship and your own well-being. Communicating these boundaries when your loved one is stable, such as "I cannot engage in circular arguments when you are manic", helps provide a predictable environment.

The Non-Enabling Stance: During manic episodes, an individual may engage in **manic spending or risky behavior** due to a temporary loss of impulse control. Loving them means refusing to enable these behaviors (e.g., not lending money for impulsive purchases) while remaining emotionally supportive. This helps minimize the "aftermath" of an episode, such as financial or legal consequences.

Education as Empowerment: Educating yourself about the disorder, understanding the difference between a "personality trait" and a "symptom", reduces frustration and helps you depersonalize difficult behaviors. When you see a symptom rather than a choice, it is easier to respond with patience.

Securing Your Own Support: Being a primary support person for someone with bipolar disorder can lead to "anticipatory dread" and caregiver burnout. Seeking your own therapy or support groups is essential. It ensures that you remain a "steady anchor" rather than being pulled into the emotional turbulence of your loved one's cycles.

Borderline Personality Traits

Borderline personality traits involve intense fear of abandonment, emotional reactivity that is difficult to contain, unstable self-image, and impulsive behavior during distress. These patterns are frequently rooted in early attachment disruption or trauma. What looks dramatic from the outside often feels like desperation and emotional flooding from the inside.

Andre, 31

What he experiences: Andre loves deeply but panics when a text goes unanswered. A small disagreement can feel like the entire relationship is at risk. He may send multiple messages, become angry, or threaten to leave—then feel deep shame when the wave passes. He struggles with a stable sense of self.

What loved ones notice: His partner experiences the relationship as intense and unpredictable. Arguments escalate quickly. Loved ones feel like they are walking on eggshells, yet sense real suffering beneath the reactivity.

Helpful Tips

For Individuals: Navigating the Emotional Wave

Dialectical Behavior Therapy (DBT) Skills: DBT is the gold standard for managing high emotional intensity. It provides two essential categories of tools:

Emotion Regulation: Moving from a state where you are a victim of your moods to a state where you can acknowledge a feeling, understand it, and choose how to respond to it.

Distress Tolerance: Learning how to get through a high-stress moment without acting on impulses that might make the situation worse.

Early Trigger Identification: Emotional shifts in borderline traits often feel like they go from 0 to 100 instantly. By learning to **identify triggers** (like a specific tone of voice or a perceived slight) before the "wave peaks," you gain a small window of time to apply a coping skill before your logical brain is offline.

Specialized Therapy: Beyond skill-building, **attachment and trauma-focused therapies** (such as Schema Therapy or Mentalization-Based Treatment) help address the root causes of emotional instability. These approaches help you build a more stable internal identity and a sense of "secure base" that was often missing in early life.

For Loved Ones: Maintaining Stability and Boundaries

Boundaries Without Cruelty: Setting boundaries is essential for the health of the relationship, but the way they are set matters. For someone sensitive to rejection, a harsh boundary can feel like an attack. State your limits clearly and calmly: "I want to hear what you're saying, but I can't continue this conversation while there is yelling. I'm going to step away for 20 minutes."

The Non-Mirroring Principle: When a loved one's emotions escalate, it is natural to meet that intensity with your own anger or defensiveness. However, **mirroring escalated intensity** only fuels the fire. By remaining the "calm in the storm," you provide a stabilizing force that helps the other person's nervous system begin to settle.

Validation vs. Reinforcement: This is a crucial distinction. You can **validate the feeling** ("I can see that you are feeling incredibly hurt right now") without **reinforcing the behavior** (such as accepting verbal abuse or self-destructive threats). Validating the emotion makes the person feel heard, which can lower their distress, even if you disagree with their actions.

Protecting Your Wellbeing: Being close to someone with high emotional reactivity can be draining. Protecting your own mental health, through your own therapy, social support, and time away, is not selfish. It is what allows you to remain a consistent, compassionate presence in their life without becoming burnt out or resentful.

Complex PTSD

Complex PTSD develops from prolonged or repeated trauma, especially in childhood or relationships. Unlike single-event PTSD, it affects emotional regulation, identity, trust, and self-worth. The body's survival system stays activated long after the danger has passed.

Alicia, 45

What she experiences: Alicia survived years of emotional instability earlier in life. As an adult she appears confident, but if someone raises their voice, her body reacts instantly, racing heart, tight chest, even when she knows she is safe. She often feels embarrassed afterward.

What loved ones notice: Her partner initially interprets her emotional withdrawal after conflicts as avoidance. Over time, he begins understanding these are trauma responses, not deliberate behavior.

Serena, 40

What she experiences: Serena grew up with

emotional abuse and neglect. She is a high achiever at work but sabotages close relationships. She has intense reactions to perceived rejection, chronic shame, and dissociative episodes. She has been misdiagnosed multiple times.

What loved ones notice: Her partner feels like they are on a roller coaster, warmth one moment, cold withdrawal the next. The partner feels "shut out" and punished for someone else's past actions.

Helpful Tips

For Individuals: Healing the Nervous System

Trauma-Informed Modalities: Because trauma is often stored in the body and the subconscious, traditional talk therapy may not be enough.

EMDR (Eye Movement Desensitization and Reprocessing): Helps the brain reprocess traumatic memories so they lose their emotional charge.

Somatic Therapy: Focuses on releasing the physical tension and "stuck" survival energy held in the body.

IFS (Internal Family Systems): Helps you understand and heal the different "parts" of your psyche that developed to protect you during the trauma.

Grounding as a Safety Tool: When a trigger occurs, the brain can lose contact with the present moment (dissociation). Grounding techniques, like feeling your feet on the floor or naming objects in the room, help pull your nervous system back into the "here and now," signaling that you are currently safe.

Identifying the "Then" vs. "Now": Recovery involves training the brain to recognize **emotional flashbacks**. By consciously labeling a reaction as a "past trigger" rather than a "present-day threat," you reduce the power that old memories have over your current behavior and relationships.

For Loved Ones: Creating a Safe Harbor

Understanding the Survival Brain: Learning about **triggers and dissociation** is essential. When a survivor pulls away or lashes out, it is often a reflexive survival response, not a personal choice. Understanding the "mechanics" of trauma helps you stay calm rather than becoming defensive.

The "Safe Harbor" Concept: Your primary role is to provide a consistent, non-judgmental environment. By not taking **defensive reactions personally**, you break the cycle of conflict and show the survivor that their trauma-driven responses won't cause them to lose your support or love.

Rebuilding Trust through Specialized Help: Trauma can deeply fracture the "we-ness" of a relationship. **Couples therapy with a trauma-informed lens** provides a structured space to navigate these triggers together. It helps the partner understand the survivor's "internal map" while giving the survivor a safe way to express needs and rebuild the intimacy that trauma often erodes.

Depression

Depression is more than sadness. It is a persistent state of low energy, emotional numbness, loss of interest, and negative self-talk that interferes with daily life. Many people with depression continue to function outwardly while feeling internally depleted.

Daniel, 42

What he experiences: Over the past year Daniel has felt increasingly heavy and unmotivated. Mornings feel like pushing through fog. He concentrates poorly at work, laughs less, and has withdrawn from friends. He tells himself he is lazy, which deepens his shame.

What loved ones notice: His wife Maria sees him growing quieter at dinner, no longer suggesting family activities. When she asks what is wrong, he says he is "just tired." She feels concerned but unsure how to help without pushing him away.

James, 42

What he experiences: James, a father of two, sleeps ten-plus hours a day yet feels exhausted. Activities that once brought him pleasure now feel like obligations. He withdraws from his wife with short answers and blank phone-staring. He feels like a burden to his family.

What loved ones notice: His wife Sarah feels like a single parent, managing everything alone while James is "present but absent." She tries to cheer him up but his lack of response makes her feel unloved. She experiences deep loneliness and guilt for being frustrated.

Clinical Note

The persistent loss of interest in previously enjoyed activities is called anhedonia, a hallmark of depression. Caregivers often misinterpret depressive withdrawal as personal rejection. Psychoeducation helps families understand that depression is a physiological state, not a choice.

Helpful Tips

For Individuals: Rebuilding the Foundation

Small Daily Actions: When in a depressive state, the "mountain" of daily life feels insurmountable. By focusing on **small, manageable actions**, such as getting out of bed or taking a five-minute walk, you begin to break the cycle of inactivity. These small wins provide a subtle shift in brain chemistry and help rebuild a sense of agency.

Biological Consistency: Depression often disrupts the body's internal clock. Maintaining **consistent sleep and meal routines** acts as a physiological anchor. Providing your body with predictable nourishment and rest helps stabilize the underlying biological systems that regulate mood and energy.

Early Professional Support: Because depression can lead to "foggy thinking" and a sense of hopelessness, seeking help early is vital. A **telehealth appointment** or a brief consultation is a low-barrier way to start. It provides a professional perspective that can help distinguish between temporary burnout and a clinical condition, offering a roadmap for recovery before a crisis occurs.

For Loved Ones: Supporting the Person, Not Fixing the Problem

Empathy Over Correction: It is natural to want to offer solutions or point out "all the good things" in a person's life, but this often feels like a **correction** of their reality. **Expressing concern with empathy**, simply saying "I can see how much you're struggling, and I'm here with you", validates their experience and reduces the isolation that depression creates.

Avoiding Minimization: Phrases like **"just cheer up"** or "it's not that bad" are unintentionally harmful. They imply that the person is choosing their state or isn't trying hard enough. Avoiding these comments prevents the individual from feeling the need to "mask" their symptoms, which only leads to further depletion.

Encouragement Without Pressure: You can **encourage professional help** without making it a demand or an ultimatum. High-pressure tactics can trigger a withdrawal response in someone who is already feeling overwhelmed. Instead, offer to help with the logistics, like finding a provider or sitting in the room during a call, to lower the effort required to take that first step.

Preventing Caregiver Burnout: Supporting someone with depression is emotionally taxing. **Watching for your own burnout** is a necessary part of being a good supporter. If you become depleted, irritable, or hopeless yourself, you lose the ability to be a steady anchor. Maintaining your own boundaries and seeking your own support ensures you can remain present for the long term.

If depression becomes so severe that it leads to thoughts of suicide or self-harm, please reach out for immediate support by calling or texting the

988 Suicide & Crisis Lifeline at 988, or by using the resources listed in our Crisis Resources section.

Eating Disorders

Eating disorders are rarely just about food. They often involve attempts to regulate overwhelming emotions, perfectionism, fears around control and self-worth, and deep shame. They carry the highest mortality rate of any psychiatric condition.

Rachel, 27

What she experiences: Rachel calculates food intake from the moment she wakes. Restricting gives her a sense of control. By evening, restriction catches up, she binges in secret, then floods with shame. She avoids social eating and criticizes her body relentlessly. The cycle repeats daily.

What loved ones notice: Her roommate sees increasing rigidity around food, excuses about having already eaten, and mood changes tied to eating patterns. Friends sense this is more than dieting but feel unsure whether to say something.

Zoe, 22

What she experiences: Zoe feels a rush of control when she skips meals. She counts every calorie and sees a body in the mirror that is never thin enough, despite hair loss and an irregular heartbeat. Her denial prevents her from acknowledging the severity.

What loved ones notice: Zoe's mother Elena watches her move food around her plate in silence, terrified of saying the wrong thing. She has stopped cooking family meals entirely. The household revolves around Zoe's relationship with food.

Clinical Note

Families benefit from "externalization", viewing the disorder as a separate entity from their loved one. This allows the family to fight the illness together rather than fighting each other.

Helpful Tips

For Individuals: Addressing the Root Function

Specialized Early Intervention: Eating disorders carry significant physical and psychological risks. Seeking specialized treatment early, working with professionals who understand the specific nuances of disordered eating, is the most effective way to interrupt the cycle before it becomes more deeply ingrained.

De-Shaming through Functionality: It is common to feel intense shame about these behaviors, but it is helpful to recognize that the behavior originally developed to **serve a function**. Whether it provides a sense of control, numbs painful emotions, or acts as a form of self-punishment, understanding the "why" allows you to address the underlying need with healthier tools rather than just fighting the symptom.

Integrated Recovery: Healing requires a dual approach. You must work with providers who address both **emotional and nutritional recovery**. Focusing only on food ignores the psychological drivers, while focusing only on emotions may neglect the urgent physical stabilization the body needs to function and think clearly.

For Loved Ones: Focusing on the Person, Not the Body

Remove Appearance from the Conversation: Even well-intentioned comments like "you look healthy" or "you've lost weight" can be misinterpreted by the eating disorder as a reason to continue or escalate behaviors. **Avoiding all comments on weight or appearance** helps shift the focus away from the body and back toward the person's internal experience.

Behavioral vs. Visual Concern: When expressing worry, focus on **behaviors and over-all wellbeing** rather than physical looks. Mentioning things like "I've noticed you seem more withdrawn lately" or "I'm concerned about your energy levels" is more helpful and less triggering than pointing out physical changes.

Encouragement Without Monitoring: Your role is to be a source of support, not a **food monitor**. Constantly watching what the person eats, counting their calories, or hovering during meals can create an environment of surveillance that increases their anxiety and secrecy. Encourage them to follow their professional treatment plan while you focus on being a steady, non-judgmental emotional presence.

Excessive Gaming in Adolescents

Gaming itself is not inherently unhealthy. The concern arises when it replaces sleep, school, real-world relationships, hygiene, and emotional balance. Excessive gaming often reflects a need for escape, ADHD-related reward-seeking, social anxiety, or low real-world confidence.

Ethan, 15

What he experiences: What began as fun after homework became Ethan's primary coping strategy. Inside the game he feels competent and socially connected. Outside, he feels criticized, behind at school, and disconnected from family. Reducing gaming feels harder than expected.

What loved ones notice: His parents see declining grades, late-night wakefulness, irritability when not gaming, and increasing family isolation. Arguments about screen time become frequent. Stricter limits often escalate the conflict.

Helpful Tips

For Teens: Regaining Agency Over the Game

Mood and Sleep Awareness: Gaming often masks underlying feelings of boredom, stress, or inadequacy. By paying attention to how you feel after a long session, whether you feel energized or actually more drained and irritable, you can start to see the "emotional cost" of excessive play. Protecting sleep is especially critical, as late-night gaming disrupts the brain's ability to regulate emotions the following day.

Structured Windows: Moving from "playing until I'm forced to stop" to "playing during a set window" helps transition gaming back into a choice rather than a compulsion. This structure reduces the "drag" gaming has on other parts of your life, like schoolwork or physical health.

Offline Competence and Connection: The primary draw of gaming is often the feeling of being "good" at something and part of a team. Finding offline activities that provide a similar sense of mastery (like sports, music, or a job) and connection helps reduce the "pull" of the virtual world by making the real world feel more rewarding.

For Parents: Shifting from Conflict to Collaboration

Balance Over Punishment: Approaching gaming as a "bad behavior" to be punished often leads to secrecy and power struggles. Instead, frame the conversation around **balance**. The goal isn't to take away their joy, but to ensure that gaming isn't "crowding out" essential developmental needs like sleep, movement, and face-to-face social interaction.

Curiosity About the "Why": Stay curious about what your teen is getting from the game. Are they leading a team? Are they escaping a lonely school day? Are they finally feeling successful at something? Understanding the **emotional function** of the game allows you to address the root need rather than just fighting over the screen time.

Predictable Limits: Ambiguous rules create constant negotiation and anxiety for the teen. Setting clear, predictable limits, and sticking to them, provides a sense of security. When a teen knows exactly when they can play and for how long, they are less likely to feel they have to "fight" for every minute.

Assessing Underlying Drivers: Excessive gaming is frequently a "symptom" rather than the primary problem. It is often used to self-medicate for **ADHD** (seeking dopamine), **Anxiety** (seeking a predictable environment), or **De-**

pression (seeking a distraction from numbness). Assessing for these underlying issues ensures you are treating the cause and not just the behavior.

Gambling Addiction

Gambling addiction involves craving the rush of risk and reward, chasing losses, escalating secrecy, and repeated unsuccessful attempts to stop. It often functions as emotional escape or a way to temporarily feel hopeful and in control.

Brian, 40

What he experiences: What started as casual sports bets became compulsive after early wins gave Brian a surge of adrenaline and relief. Now he chases losses, hides transactions, and promises himself he will stop, but the cycle keeps pulling him back. Gambling has become tied to hope, desperation, and shame.

What loved ones notice: His partner discovers unexplained withdrawals and a lack of financial transparency. Brian becomes defensive about money. His mood swings between unusual hopefulness and irritable withdrawal. Loved ones sense something is wrong before they know what.

Helpful Tips

For Individuals: Breaking the Cycle of Risk

Specialized Addiction Treatment: Gambling affects the brain's reward system in a way similar to substance use. Seeking early intervention from professionals who specialize in behavioral addictions is essential to address the neurological and psychological patterns at play.

Barriers to Access: Because the urge to gamble can be impulsive and overwhelming, "friction" is your best ally. Using software to **block access to gambling platforms** and betting apps removes the immediate opportunity to act on an urge, providing the necessary space for your logical brain to re-engage.

Financial Accountability: Money is the "fuel" for this addiction. Involving a trusted **accountability person** to manage or oversee your finances reduces the burden of self-control. This transparency helps rebuild trust and ensures that resources are protected during the recovery process.

Addressing the Root Trigger: Recovery is rarely successful if you only focus on the gambling itself. You must **address underlying emotional triggers**, such as loneliness, chronic stress, or a sense of inadequacy, to understand what the gambling was trying to "fix."

For Loved Ones: Protecting the Foundation

Financial Protection and Limits: Your primary responsibility is to **protect the family's finances**. This may involve moving shared assets to separate accounts or setting clear limits on access to funds. Establishing these boundaries is a necessary act of safety, not a lack of trust.

The Non-Rescuing Stance: It is natural to want to pay off a loved one's debts or "fix" a legal crisis, but **rescuing often enables the behavior** by shielding the individual from the natural consequences of their actions. Allowing them to feel the weight of the situation is often the catalyst they need to seek real help.

Encouraging Community Support: Direct your loved one toward **treatment and support groups** (like Gamblers Anonymous). These environments provide a community of people who understand the specific shame associated with gambling, reducing isolation and providing a proven roadmap for change.

Prioritizing Your Own Support: Living with someone struggling with addiction is traumatic and exhausting. **Seeking support for yourself**, through therapy or groups like Gam-Anon, is vital. It ensures that you remain mentally healthy and prevents your own well-being from being entirely dictated by the highs and lows of your loved one's recovery.

Gender Identity Confusion in Adolescents

Gender dysphoria involves significant distress arising from a mismatch between how a person experiences their gender internally and how their body or social role is perceived. In teens, puberty often intensifies this discomfort. The core concern is the teen's emotional experience and level of distress, not external assumptions.

Avery, 15

What they experience: Avery has felt uncomfortable in their body for years, but puberty made it worse. Body changes others found normal feel deeply distressing. Looking in mirrors and getting dressed became emotionally complicated. Gendered words feel jarring. At school, names, pronouns, bathrooms, and peer assumptions heighten discomfort. Some days Avery feels relief imagining being seen differently; other days, confusion and shame.

The biggest burden is isolation, not only the dysphoria itself, but uncertainty about whether they will be believed or rejected.

What loved ones notice: Parents see their teen more withdrawn, sensitive about appearance, and resistant to certain clothes or gendered conversations. Increased anxiety, sadness, and avoidance of mirrors or social situations may be present. If Avery expresses a different name or pronouns, parents may react with confusion, fear, or support, and even supportive parents often go through their own adjustment process.

Helpful Tips

For Teens: Finding Space to Explore

Support: Gender identity can be complex to navigate, especially during the social pressures of high school. Seeking out **trusted support**, whether through a parent, a family member, a counselor, a support group, or a mentor, ensures you aren't carrying the weight of confusion or isolation alone.

The Permission to Explore: There is often a self-imposed pressure to have a definitive "answer" or label immediately. Giving yourself **permission to explore your identity thoughtfully** means acknowledging that identity can be a journey. You do not need to have every detail of your future or your labels figured out right away; the focus should be on what feels most authentic to you in the present.

For Parents and Loved Ones: Prioritizing the Relationship

Calm, Curious Care: A teen sharing their experience of gender identity confusion is an act of profound trust. Responding first with **calm and curiosity** rather than panic or judgment keeps the lines of communication open. Asking open-ended questions about their experience shows that you are a partner in their wellbeing rather than an obstacle to it.

Avoiding Dismissal: It is crucial to **avoid mocking or dismissing** the experience. Even if the teen's identity continues to evolve, the distress they feel in the moment is real. Dismissal can lead to withdrawal and increased risk for mental health struggles.

Professional and Emotional Safety: If the experience is causing significant distress, seek out **competent mental health support**. A specialist can help navigate the complexities of identity while you focus on **prioritizing emotional safety**. This is especially vital if the teen is showing signs of anxiety, depression, or self-harm, as supportive family environments are one of the strongest protective factors against these risks.

Grief

Grief is the natural response to loss. Prolonged grief disorder, now recognized in the DSM-5-TR, occurs when the grieving process becomes persistent and debilitating, significantly impairing functioning months or years after a loss.

Patricia, 58

What she experiences: Eighteen months after losing her husband of thirty years, Patricia cannot enter certain rooms, breaks down at his favorite songs, and has stopped attending social gatherings. Her adult children worry she is "stuck."

What loved ones notice: Her daughter Elena feels she has "lost both parents", one to death and one to unending sorrow. The family visits less because the atmosphere is heavy, which increases Patricia's isolation.

Helpful Tips

For Individuals: Moving Through the Fog

Targeted Therapeutic Support: Standard talk therapy may not fully address the complexities of persistent loss. **Grief-focused Cognitive Behavioral Therapy (CBT)** is designed to help you process the trauma of the loss, manage the intrusive memories, and gradually re-engage with life without feeling like you are leaving the deceased behind.

Biological Assistance: In some cases, the emotional weight of prolonged grief can lead to clinical depression. **Antidepressant medication** can help stabilize brain chemistry, providing enough of a "floor" for you to engage more effectively in the hard work of therapy.

Telepsychiatry and Accessibility: Grief often saps the energy required to leave the house or navigate a clinic. **Telepsychiatry** removes these physical barriers, allowing you to reintroduce professional support from the safety and comfort of your home. This can be a vital first step for those whose grief has led to significant social withdrawal.

For Loved Ones: Navigating the Complexities of Loss

The "Betrayal" Narrative: One of the hardest parts of grieving is the internal feeling that experiencing joy or "moving toward life" is a betrayal of the person who died. Helping a loved one understand that **their survival and**

growth are not a rejection of the deceased is a powerful act of permission that can help unlock a stalled mourning process.

Specialized Care: If you notice that a loved one's grief is not shifting over time, **encourage specialized grief therapy**. General support is helpful, but specialists are trained to identify the "stuck points" that keep someone in a state of acute mourning long after the event.

Addressing "Stalled Mourning" in Yourself: Supporting someone in deep grief can lead to your own emotional paralysis. It is essential to **seek support for your own "stalled mourning"** or caregiver burnout. If you are also stuck in the past to maintain a connection with the grieving person, you cannot be the anchor they need to find their way back to the present.

LGBTQ+ Stress Related to Rejection, Concealment, and Identity Strain

LGBTQ+ mental health strain often arises not from identity itself, but from the chronic burden of concealment, fear of rejection, stigma, and environments where belonging feels conditional. This is often described as minority stress.

Luis, 23

What he experiences: Luis has known he is gay for years but has not fully come out. Around family, coworkers, and his religious community, he constantly calculates what to say and what to hide. Ordinary conversations require editing. He monitors his voice, mannerisms, and social media more than anyone realizes. He feels lonely even when surrounded by people, physically present, but not fully known. He sometimes internalizes negativity around him, even though he knows intellectually nothing is wrong with who he is.

What loved ones notice: Close friends see Luis more relaxed and authentic in accepting settings, but guarded and careful around family. He carries anticipatory anxiety before gatherings and becomes drained in environments where he must self-monitor. Less aware family members may assume he is simply private or moody, not realizing how much energy goes into hiding.

Helpful Tips

For Individuals: Healing from the Burden of Concealment

Seeking Integrated Belonging: "Splitting yourself" occurs when you feel forced to hide certain parts of your identity to remain safe or accepted in specific spaces (like work, family, or religious circles). Finding **affirming spaces** where your whole self is welcome allows your nervous system to exit "survival mode" and experience true belonging.

The Cost of Protective Concealment: It is important to recognize that hiding your identity (concealment) is often a **protective strategy** developed to avoid rejection or harm. However, maintaining this "mask" is emotionally expensive; it leads to chronic anxiety and a sense of being "physically present but not fully known." Acknowledging this cost is the first step toward reclaiming your energy.

Affirming Mental Health Support: Traditional therapy may not always account for the specific nuances of minority stress. Working with **LGBTQ-affirming providers** ensures that your experiences with identity strain, stigma, and self-worth are validated rather than pathologized. This specialized support helps untangle internalized negativity from your true sense of self.

For Loved Ones: Moving from Tolerance to Affirmation

Unconditional Acceptance: Support should not be a negotiation. **Do not make acceptance conditional** on how "comfortable" you feel, how "fast" the individual is moving, or whether they express their identity in a way you find traditional. Real support requires prioritizing the individual's authenticity over your own convenience or timing.

Affirmation vs. Tolerance: There is a profound difference between "putting up with" someone (tolerance) and actively valuing them (affirmation). **Being tolerated** still feels like a form of rejection because it implies that the person's identity is a burden to be managed.

Affirmation means celebrating the person as they are.

Creating Emotional Safety: Safety is built through **consistency and language**. Speaking up against anti-LGBTQ+ rhetoric even when the person isn't in the room, and maintaining an open, curious attitude creates an environment where the individual doesn't have to "scan for danger" before being themselves. These actions prove that your home or relationship is a reliable sanctuary.

Marital Conflict

Marital conflict often begins not with a lack of love, but with repeated misattunement, unresolved resentment, different conflict styles, and emotional loneliness. Many couples fall into a pursuer-distancer dynamic where one seeks engagement while the other withdraws to self-protect.

Jasmine & Mark

Her experience: After eighteen years of marriage, Jasmine feels emotionally lonely. When she raises concerns, her husband defends himself or withdraws. She stops bringing things up, becomes irritable and resentful, and misses feeling that her feelings matter.

His experience: Mark knows Jasmine is unhappy but feels confused and criticized. When she says "I miss you," he hears "you're failing." He shuts down to prevent escalation, but Jasmine experiences this as emotional withdrawal. Neither feels understood.

Helpful Tips

For Couples: De-Escalating the Cycle

Slowing Down the Interaction: In the heat of an argument, the nervous system often goes into a "threat response," making it impossible to process complex emotions. By intentionally **slowing conversations down**, you allow space for the logical brain to stay engaged. Shifting the focus from **complaints** (what the other person did wrong) to **feelings** (how the situation affects you) reduces the likelihood of the other partner becoming defensive.

The "Always" and "Never" Trap: Using absolute language like **"always" and "never"** is often inaccurate and feels like a character attack. This usually triggers a counter-attack rather than a resolution. Removing these terms keeps the conversation focused on a specific, solvable issue rather than a broad condemnation of a partner's personality.

The "Low-Arousal" Rule: Attempting to solve deep-seated issues while angry is rarely productive. **Discussing issues when calm** ensures that both partners have the emotional bandwidth to be curious about the other's perspective rather than just trying to "win" the argument.

Breaking Long-Standing Patterns: Many couples fall into a "pursuer-distancer" dynamic, where one person seeks engagement and the other withdraws to protect themselves. **Couples therapy** provides a neutral third party to help identify these invisible "dances" and provides new tools to break patterns that may have been repeating for years.

For Each Partner: Developing Self-Awareness

Identifying Conflict Styles: Everyone enters a relationship with a "conflict style" often learned in childhood, some people yell, some shut down, and some try to fix things immediately. **Learning your own style** allows you to take responsibility for your part of the dynamic and notice when your "default" reaction is making the situation worse.

Accessing "Softer" Emotions: Beneath anger, criticism, or defensiveness, there is usually a **softer emotion** like hurt, fear, or loneliness. For example, a criticism like "You're always late!" often hides a softer feeling like "I feel unimportant when I'm left waiting." Practicing the vulnerability required to share the softer emotion is often what finally reaches a partner.

The Dual Pain of Conflict: It is helpful to remember that **feeling blamed and feeling unheard** are both deeply painful experiences. When you recognize that your partner's defensiveness might be a reaction to feeling blamed, or their anger might be a reaction to feeling unheard, it becomes easier to move toward empathy and away from combat.

Midlife Emotional Strain in Men & Women

Midlife distress in men is often underrecognized because it may not look like obvious sadness. It may present as withdrawal, irritability, overwork, boredom, numbness, or avoidance. Because many men are socialized to suppress vulnerability, their strain may go unnoticed until it affects mood, relationships, health, or coping behaviors.

Marcus, 52

What he experiences: Marcus has always been dependable, raised to handle responsibilities and not complain. But lately he feels a heaviness he cannot name. He notices his body slowing, younger colleagues entering his field, and the second half of life approaching fast. His marriage is functional but not emotionally connected. Work no longer gives him the same identity or energy. He wonders: "Is this what the rest of my life feels like?" His distress shows up as irritability, restlessness, emotional withdrawal, and numbing through screens and busyness.

What loved ones notice: His wife sees him more distant, easier to frustrate, and harder to reach. He spends more time alone, talks less about feelings, and seems either preoccupied or emotionally flat. Family assumes he is simply stressed or grumpy, not recognizing deeper emotional strain.

Helpful Tips

These strategies address **Midlife Emotional Strain in Men**, a period often characterized by a transition in identity, purpose, and physical vitality. Because men are often socialized to lead with strength and stability, this internal shift can frequently manifest as quiet withdrawal or irritability rather than outward sadness.

For Individuals: Expanding the Internal Narrative

Broadening Emotional Literacy: Many men default to descriptors like **"stressed" or "tired"** to cover a wide range of complex feelings. Expanding your vocabulary allows you to identify more specific states, such as feeling overlooked, redundant, bored, or grieving a past version of yourself. Naming the specific emotion is the first step toward managing it.

Addressing the "Midlife Questions": It is common to experience an existential "reckoning" regarding one's achievements and the path ahead. Rather than **numbing these questions** through overwork, substances, or digital distractions, taking them seriously allows for a more intentional second half of life.

Diversifying Identity: For many, professional success has been the **only stable identity source** for decades. If work is the only place you feel "needed" or "competent," any shift in your career can feel like a total loss of self. Developing identities as a mentor, hobbyist, friend, or community member creates a more resilient emotional foundation.

Finding Shared Language: Group settings like **therapy, coaching, or men's groups** are effective because they break the isolation of midlife. Hearing other men articulate similar struggles provides the "language" and permission needed to process your own experience without shame.

For Loved Ones: Looking Past the Silence

The Myth of "Fine": In many traditional dynamics, a man's silence is interpreted as contentment or "having things under control." However, you should **not assume silence means everything is fine**. Often, the most profound emotional labor is happening internally while the person remains outwardly quiet.

Recognizing the Symptoms of Strain: Emotional distress in men often "leaks" out through **withdrawal, irritability, and numbness**. If a loved one is suddenly more frustrated by minor inconveniences or seems "checked out" even when present, these may be signs of a nervous system that is overextended and struggling to cope.

Inviting Without Pressuring: The goal is to open a door without forcing the person through it. **Invite conversation** with open-ended observations rather than accusations. Phrases like, "I've noticed you've been a bit quieter lately and I'm wondering how you're doing," allow the individual to share at their own pace without feeling pressured to "perform" or shamed for their struggle.

Midlife Emotional Strain in Women

Midlife for many women is not only hormonal, it is psychological, relational, and existential. After years of caregiving, overfunctioning, and self-sacrifice, long-silenced needs may become impossible to ignore. What looks like irritability from the outside may be grief, depletion, awakening, and a need for redefinition.

Denise, 49

What she experiences: Denise spent her adult

life being responsible for everyone else, career, children, household, aging parents. Now her children need her differently, her body is changing, sleep is inconsistent, and she feels more emotionally raw. She finds herself asking: "Who am I when I'm not taking care of everyone else?" She feels proud of what she built, yet also feels grief, restlessness, and resentment she cannot easily explain. She has less tolerance for emotional neglect and is more aware of imbalances she once suppressed.

What loved ones notice: Her husband sees her more easily frustrated, more direct, and less accommodating. Her children notice she seems more tired and less endlessly available. Friends hear her talking about burnout, purpose, and the fear of becoming invisible. Some misread these changes as "just menopause," but Denise is not simply more emotional, she is becoming more aware.

Helpful Tips

For Individuals: Honoring the Transition

Beyond "Just Hormones": While biological changes are real, dismissing your experience as "just hormones" can be a form of self-gaslighting. It is important to **assess sleep, mood, and burnout honestly**. Often, the irritability or sadness experienced is a valid response to years of overfunctioning and accumulated stress, now amplified by physiological shifts.

Prioritizing Personal Needs: Midlife often brings a "reckoning" with self-sacrifice. Creating space to ask **what you need now**, rather than focusing solely on what others need from you, is essential for mental health. This isn't about being "difficult"; it's about establishing a sustainable way of living for the second half of life.

Holistic Support: Because this stage is both physical and emotional, support should be integrated. Seeking help that addresses **both aspects of midlife**, such as a combination of medical consultation (for sleep or cycle changes) and therapy (for identity and burnout), ensures that you are treating the whole person rather than just a set of symptoms.

For Loved Ones: Adapting to Changing Needs

Avoid Minimization: Phrases that suggest a loved one is "just being emotional" or "going through the change" are deeply minimizing. They ignore the profound psychological work often happening during this time. Validating that her experience is complex and real helps maintain the emotional bond.

Understanding "Increased Sensitivity": What may look like a sudden drop in patience is often the result of **accumulated strain**. As her needs and capacity shift, she may no longer be able to absorb the emotional labor she once did. Recognizing this as a shift in "bandwidth" rather than a personal attack helps you stay connected.

Curiosity Over Defensiveness: When she expresses frustration or a need for change, the most helpful response is **curiosity**. Asking, "Can you help me understand what you're feeling right now?" or "What would support look like for you today?" moves the dynamic from a conflict to a partnership. It shows that you are willing to adapt alongside her as she navigates this transition.

Mood Swings

Mood instability involves unpredictable shifts between energy and discouragement, often influenced by stress, sleep disruption, emotional regulation challenges, or underlying mood disorders.

Trevor, 29

What he experiences: Some mornings Trevor feels energized and optimistic; other days he wakes irritable and overwhelmed by small frustrations. The unpredictability frustrates him, "Why can't my mood just stay stable?"

What loved ones notice: His girlfriend sees his mood shift within days, from enthusiasm about future plans to withdrawn silence. She feels unsure how to respond.

Helpful Tips

For Individuals: Stabilizing the Internal Rhythm

Biological Consistency: Mood stability is

closely tied to the body's circadian rhythm. **Maintaining consistent sleep routines**, going to bed and waking up at the same time every day, helps regulate the hormones and neurotransmitters that govern your emotional baseline.

Identifying Patterns: Because mood shifts can feel random, **tracking your mood** is essential. By noting your energy levels alongside daily events, you can begin to identify specific "triggers," such as certain social interactions, dietary habits, or work stressors, that precede a shift.

Determining the Need for Care: It is important to recognize when shifts move beyond "normal" irritability. **Seeking a professional evaluation** is recommended if these swings begin to interfere with your ability to maintain relationships, perform at work, or manage daily responsibilities.

For Loved Ones: Being a Predictable Anchor

Depersonalizing the Shift: When a loved one suddenly becomes withdrawn or irritable, it is natural to feel targeted. However, **avoiding taking mood shifts personally** allows you to remain objective. Recognizing the shift as a symptom of emotional dysregulation rather than a reflection of your relationship helps prevent unnecessary conflict.

Supportive Encouragement: You can play a vital role by **encouraging tracking and professional assessment**. Rather than diagnosing them, suggest tools (like a mood app) or a check-up as a way to help them regain a sense of control over their own wellbeing.

Predictability as a Tool: For someone experiencing internal turbulence, an unpredictable environment is a major stressor. By **offering steady, predictable support**, remaining calm and consistent in your own reactions, you provide the "emotional scaffolding" they need to feel safe while they navigate their fluctuating moods.

Navigating Undiagnosed Symptoms

The period before a diagnosis is often the most isolating. Without a name for what is happening, individuals blame themselves and loved ones feel powerless. Recognizing that a persistent behavioral change is a valid reason for professional consultation, rather than waiting for a crisis, is critical.

Mark & Elena

The loved one's experience: Mark has noticed his wife Elena hasn't been herself for nearly a year, more irritable, withdrawn, disengaged. There is no crisis, just a growing emotional distance. Without a diagnosis, he feels he has no "right" to suggest a doctor, creating guilt and suppressed resentment.

The individual's experience: Elena feels like she is drowning in fog she cannot explain. She doesn't feel "unstable" but everything feels heavy. She tells herself she is weak or lazy. She stays up late hoping to feel productive, only to wake more exhausted. She fears a professional will confirm she is simply failing at life.

Clinical Note

Many individuals endure years of silent suffering because they believe their symptoms "aren't bad enough" for a clinical label. Shifting from "internal failure" to "manageable symptoms" is the most important step toward recovery.

Helpful Tips

For Individuals: Moving from Self-Blame to Frameworks

Deserving Care Without a Crisis: Many people delay seeking help because they feel their symptoms "aren't bad enough." It is important to recognize that **you do not need a crisis to deserve an evaluation**. Waiting for a total breakdown only prolongs suffering; seeking help early allows you to address issues while you still have the functional capacity to engage in the process.

The Power of a Professional Framework: When you are struggling without a diagnosis, it is easy to view your difficulties as "internal failures" or "laziness." A professional evaluation provides a clinical **framework** that externalizes the problem. This shift allows you to **stop**

self-blame and see your struggles as manageable symptoms with a specific, **targeted path forward**.

Lowering the Barrier with Telehealth: The logistical and emotional weight of going to a clinic can be a major barrier when you are already feeling depleted. **Telehealth makes this step easier** by allowing you to access a high level of care from a private, familiar environment, reducing the "activation energy" required to start.

For Loved Ones: Suggesting Support with Clarity and Care

Validating the Need for Support: You do not need to wait for a medical emergency to speak up. A **persistent change in behavior**, such as a long-term shift in mood, social withdrawal, or loss of interest, is a valid and compassionate reason to **gently suggest professional support**. Trusting your observations can help your loved one get help before a situation escalates.

A Low-Pressure Entry Point: One of the biggest hurdles to seeking help is the **stigma of a traditional clinical setting**. Recommending **telehealth** offers a low-pressure way for your loved one to **gain clarity** without the perceived "intensity" of an in-person psychiatric office. It frames the consultation as a simple conversation rather than a daunting medical event, making it much easier for them to agree to a first step.

Obsessive-Compulsive Disorder (OCD)

OCD involves intrusive, distressing thoughts (obsessions) and repetitive behaviors or mental rituals (compulsions) performed to reduce anxiety. The cycle, intrusive thought - anxiety - compulsion - temporary relief - return of doubt, strengthens over time. OCD is not about liking order; it is driven by fear.

Michael, 38

What he experiences: Michael checks locks, stoves, and the garage repeatedly before leaving. While driving, he fears he may have hit someone without realizing it and sometimes drives back to check. He knows this is irrational but the uncertainty feels unbearable. By evening he is mentally exhausted.

What loved ones notice: His partner sees that simple routines take far too long. She realizes the checking is driven by distress, not preference. Reassurance helps briefly but the fear always returns. She feels torn between comforting him and feeling trapped.

Priya, 26

What she experiences: Priya, a teacher, spends two hours every morning checking appliances. She photographs each one for proof but still returns home to check again. She tells no one because she is ashamed. The rituals keep escalating.

What loved ones notice: Her partner Mark waits in the car each morning. He has started doing checks himself, which only makes Priya's need to check worse. He feels like an enabler rather than a partner.

Clinical Note

"Family Accommodation", where loved ones participate in rituals to reduce distress, actually fuels the OCD cycle. Emotional validation without participating in compulsions is key.

Helpful Tips

For Individuals: Breaking the Cycle of Certainty

Character vs. Thoughts: One of the most painful aspects of OCD is the nature of intrusive thoughts, which often involve themes that are the opposite of the person's true values. It is vital to recognize that **intrusive thoughts do**

not define your character. They are "ego-dystonic," meaning they are unwanted glitches in the brain's "danger detection" system, not reflections of your hidden desires or identity.

Gradual Reduction: OCD thrives on the immediate relief provided by "checking" (physical or mental). By **reducing checking gradually**, you allow your nervous system to learn that it can survive the anxiety of uncertainty without performing the ritual. This process is best done with **professional support** to ensure the pace is manageable.

Exposure and Response Prevention (ERP): This is considered the **gold-standard treatment** for OCD. It involves safely and voluntarily exposing yourself to the thoughts or situations that trigger anxiety (Exposure) while making a conscious choice not to perform the ritual (Response Prevention). Over time, this "habituation" weakens the brain's alarm response.

Medical Support: For many, **Medication (specifically SSRIs)** can be a helpful tool. These medications can help "lower the volume" of the intrusive thoughts, making it easier to engage in the challenging work of ERP therapy.

For Loved Ones: Validation Without Accommodation

The Reassurance Trap: It is natural to want to tell a loved one, "The stove is definitely off" or "You didn't hurt anyone." However, in OCD, **excessive reassurance reinforces the cycle**. It provides a temporary "fix" that prevents the individual from learning how to sit with their own doubt, ultimately making the obsession stronger the next time it appears.

Validating the Emotion, Not the Logic: You can be deeply supportive without participating in the OCD ritual. The key is to **validate the distress without validating the obsession**. For example, instead of checking the locks for them, you might say: "I can see that you are feeling incredibly anxious and certain right now, and I know how hard that is for you."

Encouraging Specialized Care: Because OCD requires specific therapeutic techniques like ERP, general talk therapy is often not enough. **Encouraging treatment with an OCD-informed clinician** ensures your loved one gets the right tools. A specialist can also help you navigate "family accommodation" and teach you how to set supportive boundaries that help the individual recover rather than stay stuck in the cycle.

Parent-Teen Conflict

Parent-teen conflict often reflects a developmental tension: the teen's need for autonomy meets the parent's need to ensure safety. The teen experiences monitoring as control; the parent experiences boundary-setting as love.

Maya, 16

Her experience: Maya feels scrutinized by her parents' questions. She is navigating friendship drama, body image, and academic stress. She wants support but not management. She becomes short, retreats to her room, and says "You wouldn't understand."

Her parent's experience: Maya's mother remembers when her daughter talked openly about everything. Now conversations end in arguments. She tightens rules out of fear, but the tighter the control, the more Maya pulls away. She feels grief for the closeness they have lost.

Helpful Tips

For Teens: Developing Proactive Communication

Respectful Autonomy: As you move toward independence, the way you ask for space matters. **Practicing asking for space respectfully**, for example, saying "I need an hour to decompress alone, but I'll come talk to you at dinner", prevents your parents from feeling shut out or alarmed.

Words vs. Withdrawal: When you feel overwhelmed or annoyed, the instinct is often to retreat or use "one-word answers." **Communicating needs with words** helps your parents understand your internal world so they don't have to guess. Telling them "I'm stressed about school and just need a break from questions" is more effective than slamming a door.

Intent vs. Impact: It is helpful to **remember that concern is not always control**. While a parent's questions may feel like a lack of trust, they are often driven by a desire to stay connected and ensure you are safe. Recognizing the underlying care can help lower your defensiveness.

For Parents: Shifting from Manager to Consultant

Curiosity Over Correction: When a teen makes a mistake or shares a different opinion, the parental reflex is often to "fix" or "correct" them. **Staying curious**, asking questions like "How did you arrive at that?" or "What was that experience like for you?", builds a bridge of understanding rather than a wall of judgment.

Safety vs. Power: To reduce conflict, it is essential to **separate safety rules from power struggles**. High-stakes issues (like substance use or physical safety) require firm boundaries, but low-stakes issues (like room tidiness or clothing choices) are often better left as areas where the teen can exercise their own judgment.

Connection Outside of Discipline: If the only time you interact with your teen is to discuss chores, grades, or rules, the relationship becomes purely transactional. **Creating connection opportunities** that have nothing to do with discipline, like a shared hobby, a drive, or just watching a show together, rebuilds the emotional bank account needed to survive the harder conversations.

The 80/20 Rule: Try to **listen more than you lecture**. Teens are much more likely to value your guidance if they feel they have been fully heard first. When they talk, your primary job is to listen and validate, not to immediately provide a "lesson."

For Families: Building a Culture of Respect

Intervention for Adversarial Cycles: If every

conversation feels like a battleground, **family therapy** can provide a neutral space to de-escalate. A therapist helps identify the "loops" you've fallen into and provides new scripts for talking to one another without the usual triggers.

The Goal of Harmony: In a healthy family, the objective is **mutual respect and emotional safety, not total agreement**. You can disagree on music, politics, or lifestyle choices while still maintaining a baseline of kindness and safety. Success is measured by how you handle the disagreement, not by whether everyone thinks the same way.

Psychosis

Psychosis involves a significant alteration in perception and reality, hallucinations, delusional beliefs, disorganized thinking, and social withdrawal. It can occur in schizophrenia, bipolar disorder, severe depression, substance use, and other conditions. Early intervention dramatically improves outcomes.

Jordan, 24

What he experiences: During his last year of college, Jordan begins feeling that people are watching him. He hears faint whispers saying his name at night. Over time, voices comment on his actions. He feels certain some social media posts are directed at him. He becomes isolated and mistrustful, afraid and ashamed.

What loved ones notice: His parents see him pausing mid-conversation, looking around suddenly, and expressing unusual beliefs about strangers watching him. They try to reason with him, but logical arguments make him feel more misunderstood.

Tyler, 20

What he experiences: Tyler hears whispered voices and believes classmates are plotting against him. He stops bathing, skips lectures, and sleeps erratically. He believes his perception is the only truth.

What loved ones notice: Tyler's father Robert sees his son arguing with invisible people. He lives in constant crisis mode, terrified and isolated by stigma. He doesn't know how to help without increasing Tyler's suspicion.

Helpful Tips

For Individuals: Prioritizing Reality and Safety

Urgent Professional Evaluation: If you begin to experience unusual perceptions, suspicious thoughts that feel "too big" to ignore, or beliefs that others find impossible, seek a psychiatric evaluation immediately. A professional can help determine if these are symptoms of a medical or mental health condition and provide a roadmap for stabilization.

Substance Avoidance: It is vital to **avoid substances**, particularly **cannabis and stimulants** (including high-dose caffeine). These substances can chemically exacerbate dopamine imbalances in the brain, potentially triggering or worsening psychotic symptoms.

The Power of Sleep: Psychosis is often preceded or worsened by severe sleep deprivation. **Prioritizing sleep** is a medical necessity; a rested brain is far more capable of distinguishing between internal thoughts and external reality.

Building a Support Circle: If possible, **involve trusted people** in your life. Having a witness you trust can provide a "reality anchor" and help you navigate the logistics of seeking care when your own perception feels unreliable.

For Loved Ones: Focusing on Connection, Not Correction

Maintain Emotional Calm: When a loved one expresses a delusional belief, your natural instinct may be to argue or "fix" their logic. However, it is essential to **stay calm and avoid aggressive arguments**. For the person experiencing psychosis, their perception is their absolute reality; arguing only increases their fear and isolation.

Shift the Goal: Your objective should be **safety and support, not winning the argument**. Instead of trying to prove them wrong, validate the emotion they are feeling (e.g., "I can see that you feel very scared right now") without necessarily agreeing with the delusion. This maintains the bond of trust needed to get them to help.

Prompt Professional Links: Encourage pro-

fessional help quickly. The sooner an individual receives specialized care, the more likely they are to recover their baseline functioning. Offer to help with the logistics of making an appointment or driving them to a clinic.

Recognizing Emergencies: You must **seek emergency help** (such as a crisis center or emergency room) if there is an immediate risk of **self-harm** or if the individual has become **unable to meet basic needs** like eating, drinking, or maintaining hygiene. In these moments, professional intervention is a necessary act of protection.

PTSD and Trauma

PTSD develops after experiencing or witnessing a terrifying event. Symptoms include intrusive re-experiencing, avoidance, negative mood changes, and hyperarousal. PTSD and substance use frequently co-occur.

Andre, 38

What he experiences: Andre, a veteran, flinches at sudden noises, avoids crowds, and has recurring deployment nightmares. He becomes irritable over minor disagreements and self-medicates with alcohol. He feels trapped between who he was and who he has become.

What loved ones notice: His partner Chloe lives in "secondary trauma", scanning restaurants for exits, avoiding hosting friends. Her social life has disappeared. The weight of being his sole emotional anchor affects her own sleep and sense of safety.

Helpful Tips

These guidelines are designed to address **Post-Traumatic Stress Disorder (PTSD)**, a condition that can develop after experiencing or witnessing a terrifying event. PTSD affects the nervous system's ability to return to a state of calm, often leaving the individual in a cycle of intrusive memories and heightened physiological arousal.

For Individuals: Utilizing Modern Recovery Tools

Evidence-Based Interventions: Recovery from PTSD is significantly improved by targeted, researched treatments.

EMDR (Eye Movement Desensitization and Reprocessing): This therapy helps the brain reprocess traumatic memories so they are no longer experienced as current threats, reducing their emotional and physical charge.

Medication Management: Psychiatrists may prescribe medications (such as SSRIs) to help manage the intense anxiety, sleep disturbances, or depression that often accompany PTSD, creating a more stable foundation for therapeutic work.

The Benefit of Virtual Care: For many survivors, traditional clinical settings (waiting rooms, white walls, medical smells) can be inadvertent triggers that increase anxiety. **Virtual care** allows you to engage in high-level treatment from a space where you already feel safe, removing the physical barrier of a triggering environment and making consistent attendance more manageable.

For Loved Ones: Acknowledging the Shared Burden

Understanding Vicarious Traumatization: Supporting a survivor is a profound commitment that can take a toll on your own mental health. **Vicarious traumatization** occurs when a supporter begins to experience symptoms of trauma (such as intrusive thoughts, anxiety, or emotional exhaustion) through their close contact with the survivor's experiences.

Essential Self-Care: Because trauma affects the entire relational system, **having your own therapeutic support is essential, not optional**. You cannot be a "steady anchor" if your own rope is fraying. Seeking your own therapy ensures you have a dedicated space to process your feelings, maintain your boundaries, and prevent the "secondary trauma" that can lead to deep resentment or caregiver burnout.

Sex Addiction / Pornography Addiction

Compulsive sexual behavior often involves using sexual stimulation to regulate mood, escalating secrecy and shame, and emotional disconnection from real relationships. It is usually tied to stress relief, escape, or unresolved emotional pain, not simply high libido.

Kevin, 37

What he experiences: Kevin's casual pornography use became compulsive over time, a go-to escape from stress, loneliness, or emotional emptiness. He uses it even when he doesn't want to, stays up later than intended, hides browser history, and feels increasingly disconnected from real intimacy. Shame fuels the secrecy, and secrecy fuels the behavior.

What loved ones notice: His partner senses emotional distance, less openness, less spontaneity, less real intimacy. If she discovers the behavior, she may feel rejected or inadequate, though the compulsion is usually about emotional regulation, not her desirability.

Helpful Tips

These guidelines are designed to address **Post-Traumatic Stress Disorder (PTSD)**, a condition that can develop after experiencing or witnessing a terrifying event. PTSD affects the nervous system's ability to return to a state of calm, often leaving the individual in a cycle of intrusive memories and heightened physiological arousal.

For Individuals: Utilizing Modern Recovery Tools

Evidence-Based Interventions: Recovery from PTSD is significantly improved by targeted, researched treatments.

EMDR (Eye Movement Desensitization and Reprocessing): This therapy helps the brain reprocess traumatic memories so they are no longer experienced as current threats, reducing their emotional and physical charge.

Medication Management: Psychiatrists may prescribe medications (such as SSRIs) to help manage the intense anxiety, sleep disturbances, or depression that often accompany PTSD, creating a more stable foundation for therapeutic work.

The Benefit of Virtual Care: For many survivors, traditional clinical settings (waiting rooms, white walls, medical smells) can be inadvertent triggers that increase anxiety. **Virtual care** allows you to engage in high-level treatment from a space where you already feel safe, removing the physical barrier of a triggering environment and making consistent attendance more manageable.

For Loved Ones: Acknowledging the Shared Burden

Understanding Vicarious Traumatization: Supporting a survivor is a profound commitment that can take a toll on your own mental health. **Vicarious traumatization** occurs when a supporter begins to experience symptoms of trauma (such as intrusive thoughts, anxiety, or emotional exhaustion) through their close contact with the survivor's experiences.

Essential Self-Care: Because trauma affects the entire relational system, **having your own therapeutic support is essential, not optional**. You cannot be a "steady anchor" if your own rope is fraying. Seeking your own therapy ensures you have a dedicated space to process your feelings, maintain your boundaries, and prevent the "secondary trauma" that can lead to deep resentment or caregiver burnout.

Substance Use Disorder (Adults)

Substance use disorder is a medical condition characterized by compulsive use of alcohol or drugs despite harmful consequences. It involves changes in brain chemistry that affect judgment, decision-making, and self-control. Addiction is rarely about willpower alone, it is often intertwined with trauma, depression, anxiety, chronic pain, loneliness, or unresolved emotional distress.

Laura, 44

What she experiences: Laura's drinking started as a way to unwind after long workdays. Over time, one glass became a bottle. She began drinking earlier in the evening, then during the afternoon on weekends. She told herself she was managing stress, but she noticed she felt anxious and irritable without it. She has tried to cut back multiple times, sometimes for a few days, sometimes a few weeks, but stressful events pull her back. She hides bottles, minimizes how much she drinks, and feels deep shame afterward. She knows her health is being affected. She is not choosing this freely anymore; she feels trapped in a cycle where the thing that once helped her cope now controls her.

What loved ones notice: Laura's husband sees her mood become unpredictable, warm one evening, withdrawn or defensive the next. He notices empty bottles, inconsistent stories, and that she avoids events where she cannot drink. Their children sense tension but do not fully understand it. Friends have pulled back. He has tried confrontation, pleading, and silence, nothing seems to work. He oscillates between anger and grief, feeling like he is losing her to something he cannot compete with.

Derek, 38

What he experiences: Derek was prescribed opioids after a back injury. When the prescription ended, the pain remained, and so did the craving. He began finding other ways to obtain medication, then shifted to cheaper alternatives. He knows the risk. He has seen the news. But in the moment of withdrawal or emotional overwhelm, the pull feels stronger than logic. He has lost a job, strained his marriage, and feels enormous shame. He wants to stop but fears withdrawal and does not believe he can manage pain or life without it.

What loved ones notice: Derek's wife sees him increasingly secretive, financially inconsistent, and emotionally absent. He misses commitments, seems physically unwell at times, and becomes defensive or evasive when questioned. She feels frightened, angry, and helpless, unsure whether to protect him or protect herself and their children from the fallout.

Clinical Note

Addiction changes the relationship between impulse, reward, and judgment. The person is not simply making bad choices in a clear state of mind, they are caught in a compulsive cycle that distorts decision-making. Medication-assisted treatment (MAT), combined with counseling and behavioral therapy, is considered the gold standard for opioid use disorder and is effective for alcohol use disorder as well.

Helpful Tips

For Individuals: Shifting from Shame to Recovery

Early Specialized Treatment: Addiction is a complex medical condition, not a moral failure or a lack of willpower. Seeking specialized treatment early, such as detox, residential programs, or outpatient counseling, is the most effective way to interrupt the chemical cycle and begin healing the brain's reward system.

The Power of Honesty: Secrecy and isolation are the primary fuels for addiction. Being **honest with at least one trusted person** breaks the cycle of hidden use and creates an initial layer of external accountability and support.

Medication-Assisted Treatment (MAT): For many, particularly those struggling with opioids or alcohol, **Medication-Assisted Treatment** is a vital tool. Medications can help stabilize brain chemistry, reduce intense cravings, and manage painful withdrawal symptoms, providing a stable "floor" that allows you to engage more fully in the psychological work of therapy.

Addressing the "Why": Substance use often begins as an attempt to self-medicate. To achieve long-term recovery, you must **address underlying emotional pain, trauma, or co-occurring mental health conditions** (like anxiety or depression) alongside the substance use. Treating only the behavior without healing the root cause often leads to relapse.

For Loved Ones: Establishing Safety and Sanity

Prioritize Safety and Finances: When a loved one is in active addiction, your primary responsibility is to **protect your own safety and financial stability**. This may involve setting up separate bank accounts, changing locks, or establishing firm boundaries around your home to ensure that the addiction does not consume your entire life.

The Non-Enabling Stance: Loving someone with an addiction means refusing to **shield them from the natural consequences** of their choices. While it is difficult to watch a loved one struggle, "rescuing" them (by paying debts, lying to their employer, or bailouts) often removes the very discomfort that might finally motivate them to seek help.

Realistic Boundaries: You can **encourage treatment** without relying on empty threats. Avoid making **ultimatums you are not prepared to follow through on**, as inconsistent boundaries can unintentionally teach the individual that they do not need to take your limits seriously.

The Al-Anon Principle: You must **seek support for yourself** through groups like Al-Anon, Nar-Anon, or individual therapy. These resources help you process your own trauma and learn the vital lesson that **you cannot recover for someone else**. While you can offer support, you must stop participating in the destructive cycle to preserve your own mental health.

Teen Self-Harm

Self-harm in teens is usually not about wanting to die. It is often an attempt to interrupt unbearable emotional pain, numbness, self-hatred, or internal chaos. Shame leads to secrecy, secrecy increases isolation, and isolation makes the behavior more likely to recur. It should always be taken seriously because it signals significant emotional distress.

Brianna, 15

What she experiences: Brianna feels things intensely but keeps it hidden. Academic pressure, friendship conflict, and harsh self-criticism have been building. When she is overwhelmed, sad, angry, numb, panicked—she discovers that hurting herself gives brief relief. Afterward, shame floods in. She hides the behavior and worries people will think she is attention-seeking. In reality, she is trying to survive emotions too big to hold alone.

What loved ones notice: Her mother sees Brianna more withdrawn, wearing long sleeves in warm weather, and uncomfortable with personal questions. She may seem irritable or emotionally shut down. If parents discover signs of self-harm, they may react with fear, confusion, or panic, which can make the teen feel more ashamed and less likely to talk.

Clinical Note

Self-harm does not always mean the teen wants to die, but it signals significant emotional distress and can increase safety risk over time. It is often connected to overwhelming emotions, anxiety, depression, trauma, self-criticism, or difficulty expressing distress verbally.

Helpful Tips

For Teens: Moving Toward Safer Coping

Breaking the Silence: The burden of carrying self-harm alone often intensifies the emotional distress that fuels the behavior. **Telling one trusted adult**, whether a parent, school counselor, or therapist, is a brave and essential first step. It shifts the problem from a hidden struggle to a shared challenge that can be managed with support.

Identifying the "Pre-Urge" State: Self-harm often follows a specific emotional pattern. By practicing "checking in" with yourself, you can start to **identify the feelings that come be-**

fore the urge, such as intense rejection, a sense of failure, or a feeling of being "trapped." Recognizing these triggers early gives you a window of time to use different tools.

Building a New Toolkit: Moving away from self-harm requires **safer emotion-regulation tools**. With professional support, you can learn techniques to "ride the wave" of intense feelings without acting on them. This might include sensory grounding, distress tolerance skills, or finding ways to express pain through art or writing.

Redefining Strength: It is important to remember that **needing help does not make you weak**. In fact, acknowledging that your current coping strategy is no longer working and reaching out for a different path is one of the strongest things a person can do.

For Parents and Loved Ones: Prioritizing Safety and Connection

Leading with Calm Concern: Discovering that a teen is self-harming often triggers a parent's "panic response," which can lead to anger, lectures, or punishment. However, **responding with calm concern** is vital. Punishment or shame only increases the teen's distress and may drive the behavior further underground.

Safety First: Your immediate priority is **safety and emotional support**. Ensure any physical injuries are treated without judgment and focus on being a "safe harbor." Validating that they must be in significant pain to have reached this point can help lower their defenses.

Removing the Guilt: Avoid phrases that make the teen **feel guilty for upsetting others** (e.g., "Do you know what this is doing to your mother?"). Self-harm is already a shame-heavy cycle; adding the weight of others' emotions can make the teen feel like even more of a "burden," which may inadvertently increase the urge to self-harm.

Seeking Prompt Evaluation: Because self-harm signals high emotional distress and can carry escalating risks, you should **seek a prompt mental health evaluation**. This is especially urgent if there is any concern about **suicidal thoughts or escalating behavior**. A professional can help determine the underlying drivers, such as depression, anxiety, or trauma, and ensure the teen has the specialized level of care they need.

Teen Substance Abuse

Teen substance abuse is not only about poor choices. It is often also about coping, peer belonging, identity, risk-taking, and attempts to manage emotional pain. Substance use in teens can escalate quickly because the adolescent brain is still developing, especially in areas related to judgment, reward, and impulse control.

Jayden, 17

What he experiences: Jayden's substance use started socially and felt casual. Over time, the reason shifted, he began using to escape anxiety, frustration, loneliness, and emotional overwhelm. What started as occasional became frequent. He thought about it more, planned around it more, and became irritable without it. He began hiding things and lying, not out of pride, but out of fear. The substance did something for him emotionally, but the relief never lasted, and it created new problems on top of the ones he was escaping.

What loved ones notice: Jayden's father sees

his son less interested in family, more secretive, more defensive, and academically declining. He seems tired, less motivated, and emotionally unpredictable. If confronted, Jayden minimizes: "It's not a big deal." Parents feel scared, angry, and helpless. Lectures alone usually do not resolve the issue if the substance use is already functioning as emotional escape.

Helpful Tips

These guidelines address **Teen Substance Use**, where experimentation or regular use often functions as a misguided attempt to navigate the intense emotional and social pressures of adolescence. Because the teenage brain is still developing its centers for judgment and impulse control, substance use can quickly shift from a social activity to a primary, and harmful, coping mechanism.

For Teens: Taking the First Step Toward Clarity

The Power of Honesty: Carrying the secret of substance use creates a heavy burden of isolation and anxiety. **Being honest with at least one trusted adult**, whether it's a parent, a favorite teacher, or a school counselor, is the most effective way to break that cycle. It moves the situation out of the shadows and allows you to access help before the habit leads to more severe legal, social, or health consequences.

Identifying the "Why": Recovery starts with self-awareness. Try to **identify the specific feelings or situations** that trigger the urge to use. Are you trying to quiet social anxiety, escape feelings of failure at school, or simply feel like you belong? Understanding what the substance is "doing" for you emotionally helps you find healthier ways to meet those same needs.

Redefining Treatment: It is a misconception that treatment is purely about "quitting." Effective treatment is about **building better ways to cope**. It provides you with a new set of tools to handle stress and big emotions so that you eventually don't feel the need to turn to a substance for relief.

For Parents and Loved Ones: Prioritizing Evaluation Over Punishment

Seriousness Without Shame: Discovering a teen is using substances often triggers a "panic and punish" response. While the situation requires **seriousness**, reacting with **shame** often backfires, causing the teen to withdraw and hide their behavior further. Leading with concern for their wellbeing keeps the door open for honest communication.

Safety, Structure, and Evaluation: Your primary role is to provide a stable environment. Focus on **safety** (addressing immediate risks) and **structure** (clear, consistent expectations)

rather than just delivering penalties. A professional **evaluation** is essential to determine the severity of the use and to create a tailored plan for support.

Looking for Underlying Drivers: Substance use is frequently a "symptom" of an unaddressed struggle. It is vital to **assess for underlying issues** such as **ADHD, anxiety, depression, or past trauma**. Often, a teen is using a substance to "self-medicate" for these conditions. Treating the root cause is the most effective way to resolve the substance use.

Seeking Specialized Support: Adolescence is a unique developmental stage that requires a specific approach. Seek out **mental health or substance use professionals experienced with adolescents**. These specialists understand the teenage brain and can provide age-appropriate strategies that focus on long-term resilience rather than just short-term compliance.

Teens and Social Media

For many teens, social media becomes a primary environment for social comparison, identity formation, peer validation, and appearance-based self-worth. Because adolescence is already a period of heightened sensitivity to belonging and rejection, social media can intensify existing vulnerabilities.

Kayla, 16

What she experiences: Before getting out of bed, Kayla has already seen content that shapes her mood. She compares herself constantly, body, friendships, popularity. A post with lots of likes gives a temporary lift; low engagement leaves her feeling invisible. She edits photos obsessively, stays up scrolling, and uses her phone for relief from anxiety, but feels worse afterward.

What loved ones notice: Her parents see mood tied to the phone, upbeat after good interactions, tearful after disappointments. She checks notifications constantly, homework takes longer, bedtime drifts later. When told to put the phone away, she becomes defensive: "You don't understand."

Helpful Tips

For Teens: Reclaiming Your Digital Well-Being

Curate Your Feed: Pay close attention to **which accounts affect your mood**. If following certain influencers or peers consistently leaves you feeling inadequate or "less than," give yourself permission to **unfollow or mute comparison-triggering content**. Your digital space should support your mental health, not tear it down.

Diversify Self-Worth: While online engagement can feel vital, it is important to **build offline sources of self-worth**. Engaging in hobbies, sports, or creative projects where you can see tangible progress helps ground your confidence in real-world mastery.

Protect Your Rest: Limit nighttime scrolling, as the blue light and constant stream of information can disrupt sleep cycles, which are essential for emotional regulation. Remember that **likes are not a measure of value**; a digital metric cannot capture your complexity or worth as a person.

For Parents: Shifting from Monitoring to Mentoring

Prioritize Emotional Impact: Move beyond tracking hours and **ask how social media makes them feel**. Understanding the quality of their online interactions is more important than just knowing the quantity of their screen time.

Model the Behavior: Teens are highly observant of their parents' habits. **Model healthy phone boundaries** by putting your own device away during meals or family time. This creates a standard of "presence" that is more powerful than any lecture.

Holistic Support: Actively **support sleep, offline friendships, and self-esteem activities**. Providing opportunities for face-to-face connection and rest helps balance the high-stimulation nature of digital life.

Monitor for Warning Signs: Be vigilant and **watch for worsening anxiety, depression, or body image concerns**. If you notice a significant shift in their baseline mood or a preoccupation with physical perfection, it may be time to seek professional guidance.

For Families: Building a Collaborative Culture

Shared Responsibility: Instead of imposing top-down rules, **create collaborative phone boundaries**. When teens have a voice in establishing family tech "contracts," they are more likely to respect the limits.

Focus on Impact: Shift the family conversation to **focus on screen impact, not just screen time**. Discuss how digital use affects the things that matter, like the quality of your conversations, the depth of your sleep, and your ability to be mentally present with one another.

Vulnerable (Covert) Narcissistic Traits

Unlike grandiose narcissism, the vulnerable form appears more wounded, passive, and self-protective. It involves fragile self-esteem, high sensitivity to criticism, chronic feelings of being overlooked, and indirect communication of emotional needs.

Adrian, 39

What he experiences: Adrian feels sensitive, self-conscious, and underappreciated. When a colleague receives praise, he feels resentment. When his partner forgets to acknowledge something important, he experiences it as confirmation that he is unseen. Rather than stating hurt directly, he retreats into silence, sarcasm, or passive resentment.

What loved ones notice: Minor feedback upsets him disproportionately. He needs substantial affirmation but does not respond well to ordinary human imperfection. Resentment builds silently and surfaces through withdrawal or self-pity. Partners feel expected to intuitively manage his emotional state.

Helpful Tips

For Individuals: Building Internal Security

Moving from Resentment to Honesty: Vulnerable narcissism often involves "silent suffering." When you feel hurt, the instinct may be to withdraw into a "cold shoulder" or passive-aggressive behavior. Practicing **identifying hurt directly**, saying "I felt ignored when that happened", prevents that hurt from fermenting into long-term resentment and allows for actual resolution.

The Validation Loop: In this state, self-worth is often entirely dependent on **external validation**. If people aren't constantly noticing your efforts or affirming your value, your self-esteem crashes. Exploring this link helps you recognize that while praise is nice, it is an unreliable foundation for your identity.

Strengthening Internal Identity: Because the "self" feels fragile, you may feel like a victim of others' opinions. **Therapy** is a vital tool for building a more robust internal identity, one that isn't easily shattered by a missed thank-you or a minor piece of feedback.

For Loved Ones: Balancing Empathy with Boundaries

Empathy Without Overfunctioning: It is natural to want to soothe a loved one who seems constantly wounded, but **overfunctioning** (trying to anticipate and prevent every possible slight) is exhausting and ultimately unhelpful. You can offer empathy ("I'm sorry you're feeling down") without taking on the responsibility of "fixing" their mood.

Promoting Directness: When a loved one uses silence or sarcasm to show they are hurt, **encourage direct communication**. You might say, "I can tell you're upset, but I can't guess why. I'm here to listen if you can tell me directly what's on your mind."

Managing Passive-Aggressive Dynamics: It is essential to **set boundaries around passive-aggression**. If a partner is using guilt or withdrawal to control the atmosphere, you must name it and decline to participate. This prevents the relationship from becoming a cycle of emotional "detective work."

Avoiding the "Caretaker" Role: If you become a **constant emotional caretaker**, the relationship loses its balance of equality. Protecting your own emotional energy ensures that you remain a partner rather than a full-time buffer between your loved one and the rest of the world.

Part Three: The Three Pillars of Self-Care

Sleep, Movement, and Nutrition

Throughout this handbook, we have explored the language of mental health, the conditions that affect millions of people, the experiences of individuals and families navigating those conditions, and the systems designed to provide professional care. But there is one more conversation that deserves its own chapter, the conversation about what you can do for yourself, every single day, without a prescription, without a supplement, and without anyone's permission.

Mental health does not exist in a vacuum. It lives inside a body that needs to sleep, a body that needs to move, and a body that needs to be nourished. When these three foundational systems are neglected, even the best medication and therapy will struggle to reach their full potential. When they are honored, the brain and nervous system have a stronger platform from which to heal, regulate, and grow.

This chapter focuses on the three areas of daily life that you have the most direct control over and that have the greatest evidence-based impact on mental health: how you sleep, whether and how you move your body, and how you feed yourself. These are not replacements for professional care. They are the foundation that professional care builds upon.

If you are living with a mental health condition, these practices can reduce symptom severity, improve medication effectiveness, and accelerate recovery.

If you are living with someone who has a mental health condition, these practices are essential for protecting your own wellbeing and sustaining your capacity to support another person without burning out.

Pillar One: Sleep

Sleep is not a luxury. It is the single most important biological function for mental health. During sleep, the brain consolidates memories, processes emotions, clears metabolic waste, repairs neural pathways, and resets the stress response system. When sleep is disrupted, virtually every mental health condition worsens, anxiety intensifies, depression deepens, emotional regulation deteriorates, focus scatters, and the nervous system becomes increasingly reactive.

The relationship between sleep and mental health is bidirectional: poor mental health disrupts sleep, and poor sleep worsens mental health. Breaking this cycle is one of the most powerful interventions available, and it begins with habits, not pills.

The Science in Plain Language

Your brain operates on a circadian rhythm, a roughly 24-hour internal clock that tells your body when to be alert and when to wind down. This clock is primarily regulated by light exposure, meal timing, and physical activity. When your daily habits align with your circadian rhythm, sleep comes more naturally and is more restorative. When they conflict, late-night screens, irregular bedtimes, caffeine in the afternoon,the clock drifts, and sleep quality suffers.

During deep sleep, the brain's glymphatic system activates, flushing out toxic proteins and metabolic waste that accumulate during waking hours. During REM sleep, the brain processes emotional experiences from the day, which is why people who sleep poorly often feel emotionally raw, reactive, and unable to let things go. Sleep is literally where emotional regulation happens at a biological level.

Self-Care Sleep Practices

Anchor Your Wake Time

The single most effective sleep habit is waking up at the same time every day, including weekends. Your circadian clock sets itself based on when you wake and when you are exposed to light, not when you go to bed. A consistent wake time trains your body to feel sleepy at a predictable time each night. Sleeping in on weekends may feel restorative, but it shifts your clock and makes Sunday and Monday nights harder.

Get Morning Light Within the First Hour

Exposure to natural light within 30 to 60 minutes of waking is one of the most powerful circadian signals available to the human brain. Morning light suppresses melatonin, raises cortisol to a healthy waking level, and sets a timer that will trigger natural sleepiness approximately 14 to 16 hours later. Step outside for 10 to 15 minutes, even on a cloudy day, outdoor light is many times more powerful than indoor lighting. If you live somewhere with limited morning light, a 10,000-lux light therapy lamp used for 20 to 30 minutes at your wake time can serve as a substitute.

Create a Wind-Down Period

Your brain cannot go from full engagement to sleep in an instant. Begin dimming lights and reducing stimulation 60 to 90 minutes before your target bedtime. This means lowering overhead lights, avoiding intense conversations or work emails, and transitioning to calmer activities such as reading, gentle stretching, listening to music, or taking a warm bath or shower. A warm bath is particularly effective because the subsequent drop in core body temperature as you cool down signals the brain that it is time for sleep.

Manage Light and Screens at Night

Artificial light, especially the blue-spectrum

light emitted by phones, tablets, and computers, suppresses melatonin production and delays sleep onset. In the two hours before bed, dim your screens to the lowest comfortable setting, enable night mode or warm-tone filters, and ideally put screens away entirely during the final 30 to 60 minutes before sleep. If you must use a screen, keep it at arm's length and avoid content that is emotionally activating.

Keep Your Bedroom for Sleep

Train your brain to associate the bedroom with sleep, not with work, worry, or entertainment. Remove the television. Charge your phone outside the room or across the room. If you cannot fall asleep within roughly 20 minutes, get up, go to another room, do something calming, and return when you feel drowsy. This prevents your brain from learning to associate lying in bed with frustration and wakefulness.

Watch What You Consume and When

Caffeine has a half-life of five to seven hours, meaning half the caffeine from your afternoon coffee is still circulating in your system at bedtime. As a general practice, stop caffeine intake by early afternoon. Alcohol, while it may help you fall asleep initially, fragments sleep architecture and suppresses REM sleep, leading to poorer quality rest and more emotional reactivity the next day. Heavy meals close to bedtime can also disrupt sleep by requiring active digestion during a time your body should be resting.

Manage Temperature

The body needs to drop its core temperature by about one to two degrees to initiate and maintain sleep. Keep your bedroom cool, most research suggests between 60 and 67 degrees Fahrenheit is optimal. Use breathable bedding. If you run warm, consider keeping a foot or hand outside the covers, which helps the body release heat.

Handle the Racing Mind

If your mind races at bedtime, try a structured brain dump before your wind-down period: write down everything that is on your mind, tasks, worries, ideas, unresolved conversations, on paper. This is not journaling for insight; it is simply emptying the mental queue so your brain does not feel the need to keep looping. Some people also find it helpful to write a brief plan for the next day, which gives the brain permission to stop preparing and start resting.

For Caregivers and Partners

If you are living with someone whose mental health condition disrupts their sleep, and by extension, yours, protect your own sleep first. You cannot support another person from a state of chronic exhaustion. Consider separate sleep arrangements during acute periods if necessary. This is not a rejection of your partner; it is an investment in your capacity to be present and helpful. A well-rested caregiver is a more patient, more empathetic, and more effective caregiver.

Pillar Two: Movement

The human body was built to move. For the vast majority of human history, daily survival required walking, lifting, climbing, and carrying. The modern world has engineered most of that movement out of daily life, and the consequences for mental health are profound. The research is unambiguous: regular physical movement is one of the most effective interventions for depression, anxiety, ADHD, PTSD, insomnia, and overall emotional regulation, comparable in some studies to the effect of antidepressant medication for mild to moderate depression.

And yet, when people are struggling with their mental health, movement is often the first thing to go. Depression saps motivation. Anxiety creates avoidance. Exhaustion makes the couch feel like the only safe place. This is not laziness. It is the illness itself interfering with the very behavior that would help.

The goal of this section is not to prescribe a fitness regimen. It is to help you understand why movement matters for your brain, and to give you practical, realistic strategies for incorporating it into your life, even on the hard days.

The Science in Plain Language

Physical movement does several things for the brain simultaneously. It increases blood flow, delivering more oxygen and nutrients to brain tissue. It triggers the release of endorphins, serotonin, dopamine, and norepinephrine, the same neurotransmitters targeted by most psychiatric medications. It reduces cortisol and adrenaline, the stress hormones that keep the body in a state of tension and hypervigilance. It promotes neuroplasticity, the brain's ability to form new connections and adapt. And it activates the parasympathetic nervous system, helping the body shift from a state of threat into a state of calm.

In practical terms, this means that a single walk can reduce anxiety for hours. A consistent exercise habit can meaningfully reduce depressive symptoms within weeks. Regular movement improves sleep quality, sharpens focus, increases frustration tolerance, and builds a sense of agency, the feeling that you can affect your own wellbeing.

Self-Care Movement Practices

Start with Walking

Walking is the most underrated mental health intervention in existence. It requires no equipment, no gym membership, no skill, and no recovery time. A 20-30 minute walk at a moderate pace has been shown to reduce anxiety, improve mood, enhance creative thinking, and improve sleep. Walking outdoors combines the benefits of movement with natural light exposure, which further supports circadian rhythm and mood regulation. If 30 minutes feels overwhelming, start with 10. Ten minutes of walking is infinitely better than zero.

Prioritize Consistency Over Intensity

The mental health benefits of movement come primarily from regularity, not from intensity. Walking five times a week for 20 minutes will do more for your mood than one intense gym session followed by six days of inactivity. The brain responds to consistent signals. Regular movement tells your nervous system that the body is active, capable, and safe, which counteracts the shutdown signals that depression and anxiety send.

Use Movement to Regulate, Not Punish

If your relationship with exercise has been tied to punishment, guilt, appearance, or control, it is worth reframing movement as a form of care rather than a form of obligation. You are not exercising because something is wrong with your body. You are moving because your brain needs it. Choose activities that feel good, not activities that feel like penance. Dancing in your living room, stretching on the floor, playing with your children, gardening, swimming, yoga, cycling, all of it counts. The best exercise for mental health is the one you will actually do.

Pair Movement with Mood

Different types of movement serve different emotional needs. When you feel anxious or overstimulated, slow and rhythmic movement, walking, yoga, swimming, gentle stretching, helps activate the parasympathetic nervous system and bring the body out of fight-or-flight. When you feel flat, numb, or depressed, more vigorous movement, brisk walking, jogging, dancing, strength training, can help mobilize energy and activate the reward system. Learning to match your movement to your emotional state is a powerful self-regulation skill.

Build Movement Into Your Day, Not Around It

One of the biggest barriers to exercise is the belief that it has to be a separate event, a trip to the gym, a class, a run. For people struggling with mental health, the activation energy required to plan and execute a workout can feel insurmountable. Instead, build movement into what you are already doing. Walk during phone calls. Take the stairs. Park farther away. Do squats while waiting for coffee. Stretch during commercial breaks. Stand and move every hour. These micro-movements accumulate and keep the body in a state of gentle activation throughout the day.

The Five-Minute Rule

On the hardest days, commit to just five minutes of movement. Put on your shoes and walk to the end of your block. Do five minutes of stretching on the floor. The agreement is five minutes, and if you want to stop after that, you stop. What happens in practice is that once the body starts moving, the brain often follows. The hardest part is the first step. The five-minute commitment lowers the barrier enough to make that step possible.

Movement for Caregivers

If you are caring for someone with a mental health condition, your body is absorbing stress whether you realize it or not. Chronic caregiving stress manifests as muscle tension, headaches, fatigue, disrupted sleep, and a general feeling of heaviness. Regular movement is one of the most effective ways to discharge this accumulated physical stress. It is also one of the few things that is entirely yours, a space where you are not managing someone else's needs. Protect this time. It is not selfish. It is necessary.

Pillar Three: Nutrition

The connection between what you eat and how you feel is not metaphorical. It is biological. Your brain consumes roughly 20 percent of your daily caloric intake despite being only 2 percent of your body weight. It runs on glucose, requires a steady supply of amino acids and fatty acids to produce neurotransmitters, and is profoundly influenced by the health of your gut, which produces approximately 95 percent of the body's serotonin. When nutrition is erratic, insufficient, or heavily processed, the brain does not have the raw materials it needs to regulate mood, manage stress, sustain attention, or repair itself.

This section is not a diet plan. There is no calorie counting, no food restriction, and no morality assigned to what you eat. The goal is simple: understand how certain eating habits support your brain, and make small, sustainable shifts that give your nervous system the best possible foundation.

The Science in Plain Language

The gut-brain axis is a two-way communication highway between your digestive system and your brain, connected primarily through the vagus nerve. The trillions of microorganisms living in your gut, collectively called the gut microbiome, produce neurotransmitters, influence inflammation levels, and send chemical signals that directly affect mood, anxiety, and cognitive function. Research increasingly shows that gut health is not separate from mental health; it is a core part of it.

Blood sugar stability also plays a critical role. When you skip meals, your blood sugar drops, triggering cortisol and adrenaline release, the same stress hormones that fuel anxiety and irritability. When you eat highly processed, high-sugar foods, blood sugar spikes and crashes create a roller coaster of energy and mood that mimics, and worsens, anxiety and depressive symptoms. Consistent, balanced eating throughout the day provides the brain with a steady fuel supply and keeps the stress response system from being unnecessarily activated.

Self-Care Nutrition Practices

Eat Regularly

The simplest and most impactful nutritional habit for mental health is eating at consistent intervals throughout the day. Skipping meals, especially breakfast, forces the body into a stress response as blood sugar drops. Three meals a day with a snack or two in between prevents the blood sugar crashes that trigger irritability, anxiety, brain fog, and emotional reactivity. You do not need to eat perfectly. You need to eat consistently.

Eat Whole Foods More Often Than Processed Foods

Whole foods, fruits, vegetables, whole grains, legumes, nuts, seeds, eggs, fish, and lean proteins, provide the vitamins, minerals, amino acids, and fatty acids that the brain needs to produce neurotransmitters and manage inflammation. Highly processed foods, fast food, packaged snacks, sugary drinks, refined carbohydrates, provide calories without the micronutrients the brain depends on and often increase inflammation, which is increasingly linked to depression and anxiety. The shift does not need to be all-or-nothing. Each whole food meal you add displaces a processed one.

Prioritize Protein at Every Meal

Protein provides the amino acids that are the building blocks of neurotransmitters. Tryptophan (found in poultry, eggs, fish, dairy, nuts, and seeds) is the precursor to serotonin. Tyrosine (found in meat, fish, eggs, dairy, soy, and legumes) is the precursor to dopamine and norepinephrine. Without adequate protein intake, the brain cannot manufacture the chemicals it needs to regulate mood, motivation, and focus. Including a source of protein at each meal helps maintain steady energy and provides the brain with its essential raw materials.

Include Omega-3 Rich Foods

Omega-3 fatty acids, found in fatty fish such as salmon, mackerel, sardines, and trout, as well as in walnuts, flaxseeds, and chia seeds, play a critical role in brain cell structure and function. Research consistently links higher omega-3 intake with lower rates of depression and better overall brain health. Aim to include fatty fish two to three times per week, or incorporate plant-based omega-3 sources daily.

Feed Your Gut

A diverse, fiber-rich diet supports a healthy gut microbiome, which in turn supports mental health. Foods that promote gut health include vegetables, fruits, whole grains, legumes, fermented foods such as yogurt, kefir, sauerkraut, and kimchi, and prebiotic-rich foods such as garlic, onions, bananas, and oats. A gut that is well-fed with diverse fiber produces more serotonin, reduces systemic inflammation, and communicates more effectively with the brain.

Hydrate

Even mild dehydration, as little as one to two percent of body weight, can impair mood, concentration, and energy levels. The brain is approximately 75 percent water, and its function is highly sensitive to hydration status. Aim for consistent water intake throughout the day. A practical guideline is to drink enough that your urine is pale yellow. Keep water accessible, on your desk, by your bed, in your bag. If plain water feels unappealing, add a slice of lemon, cucumber, or berries for flavor.

Reduce Caffeine and Alcohol Mindfully

Caffeine is not inherently harmful, but in excess or consumed too late in the day, it amplifies anxiety symptoms and disrupts sleep, both of which worsen mental health. Pay attention to how caffeine affects your body. If you notice increased heart rate, restlessness, or difficulty sleeping, reduce your intake or set an afternoon cutoff. Alcohol, while often used to manage stress or social anxiety, is a central nervous system depressant that disrupts sleep architecture, depletes serotonin, increases next-day anxiety (sometimes called "hangxiety"), and interferes with the effectiveness of psychiatric medications. Reducing or eliminating alcohol is one of the highest-impact changes a person can make for their mental health.

Cook When You Can, and Keep It Simple

Cooking does not need to be elaborate to be nourishing. A meal of scrambled eggs with vegetables takes ten minutes. A bowl of oatmeal with nuts and fruit takes five. A simple sheet-pan dinner with protein and roasted vegetables requires minimal effort and feeds you well. When depression or anxiety makes cooking feel impossible, keep simple staples on hand: canned beans, frozen vegetables, pre-cooked grains, eggs, nut butters, yogurt, and fruit. The goal is not culinary perfection. The goal is consistently giving your brain and body something to work with.

Nutrition for Caregivers

When you are focused on caring for someone else, your own nutrition is often the first thing sacrificed. You skip meals because you are managing their crisis. You eat whatever is fast because you have no energy left to prepare food. You drink more coffee to compensate for the sleep you are losing. Over time, this pattern depletes your own neurological reserves, making you more irritable, less patient, and more vulnerable to your own mental health challenges. Feeding yourself is not optional caregiving infrastructure. Plan your meals with the same seriousness you bring to managing someone else's appointments.

Bringing the Three Pillars Together

Sleep, movement, and nutrition are not separate interventions. They are interconnected systems that amplify each other. Regular movement improves sleep quality. Better sleep improves food choices. Better nutrition provides the fuel for movement. When all three are working in reasonable harmony, the nervous system has a stable foundation from which to heal, regulate, and respond to life's challenges.

You do not need to overhaul your life overnight. Start with one small change in one pillar and build from there:

If you change nothing else, wake at the same time every day. This single habit will begin to regulate your circadian rhythm, improve your sleep, and create a stable anchor for the rest of your day.

If you change nothing else, walk for ten minutes a day. This is enough to shift neurochemistry, reduce cortisol, and remind your body that it is capable of something other than survival mode.

If you change nothing else, eat breakfast. Breaking the overnight fast with protein and complex carbohydrates stabilizes blood sugar, reduces morning anxiety, and gives your brain fuel for the first and often hardest hours of the day.

These are not glamorous interventions. They

will not go viral on social media. But they are the quiet, consistent, evidence-based habits that form the bedrock of mental health, for the person living with a condition and for the person standing beside them.

Professional care provides the clinical expertise. Medication provides the biochemical support. Therapy provides the insight and skills. But the body you live in—the one that sleeps, moves, and eats, is the vehicle through which all of that care is delivered. Take care of it.

Your habits are not a cure. They are a foundation.

Build the foundation, and give your healing somewhere strong to land.

For personalized guidance on integrating self-care practices with your psychiatric treatment plan, visit **www.VirtualPsychiatricCare.com** to schedule a consultation with a board-certified provider.

Crisis Resources

If you or someone you know is experiencing a mental health crisis, please reach out to one of the following resources immediately:

988 Suicide and Crisis Lifeline: Call or text **988**, available 24 hours a day, 7 days a week.

Crisis Text Line: Text **HOME** to **741741** to connect with a trained crisis counselor.

National Domestic Violence Hotline: Call **1-800-799-7233** or text **START** to **88788**.

SAMHSA National Helpline: Call **1-800-662-4357** for free, confidential treatment referrals and information, available 24/7.

National Alliance for Eating Disorders Helpline: Call **1-866-662-1235** for eating disorder support and referrals.

The Trevor Project (LGBTQ+ Youth): Call **1-866-488-7386**, text **START** to **678-678**, or chat at TheTrevorProject.org.

Veterans Crisis Line: Call **988**, then press **1**, or text **838255**.

Postpartum Support International (PSI): For parents experiencing maternal mental health issues. Call or text **1-800-944-4773**.

RAINN (National Sexual Assault Hotline): For survivors of sexual assault and those dealing with related trauma. Call **1-800-656-HOPE**.

Childhelp National Child Abuse Hotline: For those dealing with childhood-rooted trauma and C-PTSD. Call or text **1-800-4-A-CHILD**.

Partnership to End Addiction: A specialized helpline for parents and caregivers of teens struggling with substance abuse. Text **55753**.

National Problem Gambling Helpline: Support for those struggling with gambling addiction. Call or text **1-800-GAMBLER**.

National Mental Health Support Groups

For ongoing peer support and community connection, consider reaching out to these national organizations:

Adult Children of Alcoholics & Dysfunctional Families (ACA): A recovery program for people who grew up in dysfunctional homes. Visit ad ultchildren.org.

AL-ANON and NAR-ANON Family Groups: For families and friends of individuals struggling with substance use disorders. Visit al-anon.org or nar-anon.org.

BEAM (Black Emotional and Mental Health Collective): Black-led peer support and healing circles. Visit beam.community.

Caregiver Action Network (CAN): Provides support to family caregivers across the country. Call **1-855-227-3640** or visit caregiveraction.org.

CHADD (ADHD Support): Resources and local chapters for children and adults with ADHD. Call **1-866-200-8098** or visit chadd.org.

CPTSD Foundation Peer Support Chat Group: Moderated virtual peer support for survivors of complex trauma.

DBSA (Depression and Bipolar Support Alliance): Peer-led support groups for those living with depression and bipolar disorder. Visit dbsalliance.org.

HeadsUpGuys: A specialized resource designed to help men manage and prevent depression. Visit headsupguys.org.

Mental Health America (MHA): A wide network of affiliates and peer support resources. Visit mhanational.org.

NAMI (National Alliance on Mental Illness): Peer-led support groups for individuals and families. Call **1-800-950-NAMI (6264)** or text "**HelpLine**" to **62640**.

Red Hot Mamas: Support for midlife women dealing with menopause-related mood shifts and life transitions.

S.A.F.E. Alternatives (Self-Abuse Finally Ends): Specifically focused on helping individuals end self-injurious behavior. Call **1-800-366-8288**.

Sista Afya Community Care: Mental wellness resources and peer support specifically for Black women and girls.

Soaring Spirits International: A virtual and local community for widows and widowers.

The Dinner Party: A peer-led community for adults (ages 18–45) who have experienced significant loss.

Therapy for Black Girls / Holding Space Foundation: Culturally responsive mental health community and group healing spaces for Black women.

Trauma Survivors Network (TSN): Support groups for survivors and families through partner hospitals.

VITAS Virtual Grief Support Groups: Free remote grief and bereavement support via phone and Zoom.

Wounded Warrior Project: Programs and support for post-9/11 veterans. Call **1-877-832-6997** or visit woundedwarriorproje ct.org.

About Virtual Psychiatric Care

Virtual Psychiatric Care is a national telehealth platform co-founded by Pascale Davis, MSN, PMHNP-BC, a board-certified psychiatric nurse practitioner and Complex PTSD survivor, and Gregg Davis, a veteran brand builder and healthcare advocate with over 20 years of experience in team management and niche marketing. Together, their mission is to provide individuals and organizations with access to caring, affordable, and quality psychiatric services through convenient, secure video consultations.

Why Telehealth Is Transforming Mental Health Care

The rise of telehealth has fundamentally changed how people access psychiatric care, and the evidence is clear that virtual mental health treatment is not just a convenient alternative, but in many cases a better one.

Access Without Barriers

Geography, transportation, physical disability, and rural isolation have historically kept millions of people from receiving psychiatric care. Telehealth eliminates these barriers entirely. A person in a remote town, a homebound elderly patient, or a busy parent can now access board-certified psychiatric providers from any location with an internet connection.

Reduced Stigma and Greater Privacy

For many people, the fear of being seen entering a mental health clinic is enough to prevent them from seeking care. Telehealth removes this barrier by allowing patients to attend sessions from the privacy of their own home.

Same-Day and Walk-In Availability

Traditional psychiatric offices often have wait times of weeks or even months. Telehealth platforms like Virtual Psychiatric Care offer same-day appointments and virtual walk-in visits, meaning that help is available when the crisis is happening.

Comfort Leads to Better Outcomes

Research shows that patients who attend therapy and psychiatric appointments from their own environment often feel safer, more relaxed, and more open during sessions. This increased comfort can lead to more honest conversations, stronger therapeutic alliances, and ultimately better treatment outcomes.

Continuity of Care Regardless of Life Changes

When patients move, travel, or face life disruptions, in-person psychiatric care is often interrupted. Telehealth ensures continuity of care across state lines, during relocations, and through life transitions.

Flexible Scheduling for Real Lives

Evening and weekend appointments, no commute time, and no sitting in waiting rooms mean that telehealth fits into the lives of working professionals, parents, students, and caregivers.

Lower Cost, Greater Value

Without the overhead of physical office space, telehealth providers can often offer more affordable care. Patients also save on transportation costs, childcare, and lost wages from time off work. Many insurance plans now cover telehealth visits at the same rate as in-person care.

A Lifeline for Vulnerable Populations

Elderly individuals with mobility limitations, individuals with agoraphobia or severe social anxiety, immunocompromised patients, veterans with PTSD who find clinical environments triggering, and adolescents who resist traditional office settings all benefit enormously from the accessibility of telehealth.

Resources for Your Journey

Virtual Psychiatric Care serves as a specialized resource for those interested in exploring telehealth options. The platform focuses exclusively on mental health, offering comprehensive evaluations, ongoing medication management, and integrative therapy with licensed professionals.

You can explore these resources or schedule an initial consultation at VirtualPsychiatricCare.com

A Final Word

Mental health is not a destination; it is an on-going journey of self-discovery and resilience. By reading this handbook, you have already taken a significant step toward understanding yourself or supporting someone you love.

You are not alone in your struggle, and you do not have to navigate the path to recovery in isolation. Whether through the information in these pages, the support of your community, or the expertise of a psychiatric professional, help is within reach.

You are not alone. You are not broken. You are becoming.

VIRTUAL PSYCHIATRIC CARE

Convenient. Secure. Affordable.

www.VirtualPsychiatricCare.com

References & Data Origins

The definitions provided in the glossary are accurate summaries of established concepts in psychiatry, psychology, and modern mental health discourse. Because this list covers a vast array of topics, ranging from formal diagnostic criteria to specific therapeutic modalities and neurobiological concepts, no single source covers all of them.

Below are the primary authorities and foundational texts that serve as references for these definitions, categorized by their application within the glossary.

1. Diagnostic Systems and Mental Disorders

For definitions regarding specific diagnoses (e. g., ADHD, Bipolar Disorder, Schizophrenia, Personality Disorders, PTSD, Major Depressive Disorder), the primary authorities in the United States and globally are the American Psychiatric Association (APA) and the World Health Organization (WHO).

American Psychiatric Association. (2022). Diagnostic and statistical manual of mental disorders (5th ed., text rev.). Washington, DC: Author.

This text is the definitive source for diagnostic criteria and official definitions of mental disorders used in the U.S.

World Health Organization. (2019). International statistical classification of diseases and related health problems (11th ed.). Geneva, Switzerland: Author.

The ICD-11 provides the international standard for defining and classifying all health conditions, including mental disorders.

2. Psychotherapy Modalities and Clinical Concepts

For definitions of specific therapeutic approaches and concepts (e.g., ACT, CBT, DBT, EMDR, IFS, Polyvagal Theory), references are best drawn from the foundational texts written by the developers of these therapies or major professional organizations that set the standards for their practice.

Foundational Texts for Specific Modalities:

ACT: Hayes, S. C., Strosahl, K. D., & Wilson, K. G. (2011). Acceptance and commitment therapy: The process and practice of mindful change (2nd ed.). New York, NY: Guilford Press.

Brainspotting: Grand, D. (2013). Brainspotting: The revolutionary new therapy for rapid and effective change. Boulder, CO: Sounds True.

CBT: Beck, J. S. (2020). Cognitive behavior therapy: Basics and beyond (3rd ed.). New York, NY: Guilford Press.

DBT: Linehan, M. M. (2014). DBT skills training manual (2nd ed.). New York, NY: Guilford Press.

EMDR: Shapiro, F. (2017). Eye movement desensitization and reprocessing (EMDR) therapy: Basic principles, protocols, and procedures (3rd ed.). New York, NY: Guilford Press.

Gottman Method (referenced in Couples Therapy/Flooding): Gottman, J. M., & Gottman, J. S. (2015). 10 principles for doing effective couples therapy. New York, NY: W. W. Norton & Company.

IFS (Internal Family Systems): Schwartz, R. C., & Sweezy, M. (2019). Internal family systems therapy (2nd ed.). New York, NY: Guilford Press.

Polyvagal Theory: Porges, S. W. (2011). The polyvagal theory: Neurophysiological foundations of emotions, attachment, communication, and self-regulation. New York, NY: W. W. Norton & Company.

Window of Tolerance: Siegel, D. J. (2012). The developing mind: How relationships and the brain interact to shape who we are (2nd ed.). New York, NY: Guilford Press.

3. Neuroscience, Psychopharmacology, and Biological Concepts

For terms describing biological processes, neurotransmitters, or medication classes (e.g. , Dopamine, Neuroplasticity, Antidepressants, Vagus Nerve, ECT), standard medical and neuroscience textbooks serve as the reference authorities.

Kandel, E. R., Koester, J. D., Mack, S. H., & Siegelbaum, S. A. (Eds.). (2021). Principles of neural science (6th ed.). New York, NY: McGraw Hill.

Stahl, S. M. (2021). Stahl's essential psychopharmacology: Neuroscientific basis and practical applications (5th ed.). Cambridge, UK: Cambridge University Press.

4. Emerging Concepts and Terms in Popular Mental Health

Terms that are not formal clinical diagnoses but are widely used in modern mental health discourse (e.g., ASMR, Doom Scrolling, Toxic Positivity, Boundaries, People-Pleasing) are defined based on psychological theory, emerging research, or consensus within the professional community.

ASMR: Poerio, G. L., Blakey, E., Hostler, T. J., & Veltri, T. (2018). More than a feeling: Autonomous sensory meridian response (ASMR) is characterized by reliable changes in affect and physiology. PLOS ONE, 13(6), Article e0196645. https://doi.org/10.1371/journal.pone.0196645

Doom Scrolling: Sharma, B., Anand, N., Singh, P., & Singh, R. (2022). Doomscrolling: An exploratory study on its causes and consequences. Journal of Affective Disorders Reports, 10, Article 100412. https://doi.org/10.1016/j.jadr.2022.100412

Boundaries / People-Pleasing: These concepts are central themes in theories of codependency and family systems. A foundational reference is: Beattie, M. (1986). Codependent no more: How to stop controlling others and start caring for yourself. Center City, MN: Hazelden Information & Educational Services.

The clinical information and diagnostic criteria in this handbook are synthesized from these authoritative medical and psychological institutions:

I. Diagnostic Standards & Clinical Overview

American Psychiatric Association (APA): All diagnostic language and symptom criteria align with the Diagnostic and Statistical Manual of Mental Disorders, Fifth Edition, Text Revision (DSM-5-TR). Source: psychiatry.org

The Mayo Clinic: Used for verifying physiological symptoms and medical complications of mental health conditions. Source: mayoclinic.org

II. Neurodevelopmental & Behavioral Disorders

ADHD (Chapter 1): Clinical guidelines provided by **CHADD** (Children and Adults with Attention-Deficit/Hyperactivity Disorder). Source: chadd.org

Substance Use (Chapters 34 & 36): Statistics and treatment modalities sourced from **SAMHSA** and the **National Institute on Drug Abuse (NIDA)**. Source: samsha.gov

III. Trauma & Complex PTSD (C-PTSD)

National Center for PTSD: A division of the U.S. Department of Veterans Affairs. Source: ptsd.va.gov

CPTSD Foundation: Specialized research regarding the long-term effects of relational and complex trauma. Source: cptsdfoundation.org

The Body Keeps the Score: Theoretical foundations regarding the somatic experience of trauma by Dr. Bessel van der Kolk.

IV. Specialized Populations (Youth & LGBTQ+)

The Trevor Project: Standards for LGBTQ+ youth crisis intervention and gender-affirming care. Source: thetrevorproject.org

The Jed Foundation (JED): Clinical frameworks for teen emotional health and suicide prevention. Source: jedfoundation.org

V. The Three Pillars of Wellness

Sleep (Pillar One): Based on the **National Sleep Foundation's** "Sleep Quality Indicators." Source: thensf.org

Movement (Pillar Two): Based on the **CDC's** Physical Activity Guidelines for Americans. Source: cdc.gov

Nutrition (Pillar Three): Sourced from research on the gut-brain axis and **Nutritional Psychology**. Source: nutritional-psychology.org

Note: This handbook is for educational purposes only. For a formal diagnosis or personalized treatment plan, please consult a licensed psychiatric professional at Virtual Psychiatric Care.